MW00773700

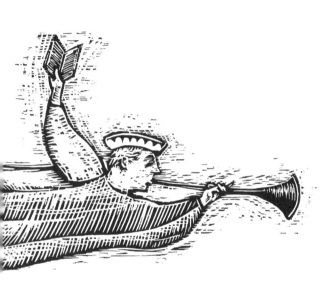

3rd, 4th Nephi: *a brief theological introduction*

This publication was made possible by generous support from the Laura F. Willes Center for Book of Mormon Studies, part of the Neal A. Maxwell Institute for Religious Scholarship at Brigham Young University.

Published by the Neal A. Maxwell Institute for Religious Scholarship, Brigham Young University, Provo, Utah. The copyright for the 2013 text of The Book of Mormon is held by The Church of Jesus Christ of Latter-day Saints, Salt Lake City, Utah; that text is quoted throughout and used by permission.

The Maxwell Institute's *The Book of Mormon: brief theological introductions* series offered by Brigham Young University is not made, provided, approved, or endorsed by Intellectual Reserve Inc. or The Church of Jesus Christ of Latter-day Saints. Any content or opinions expressed, implied, or included in or with this book are solely those of the author and are not necessarily those of Brigham Young University or any of its affiliates, Intellectual Reserve, Inc., or The Church of Jesus Christ of Latter-day Saints.

Printed in the United States of America

ISBN:978-0-8425-0018-0
LIBRARY OF CONGRESS CONTROL NUMBER: 2020902548

3rd, 4th Nephi

a brief theological introduction

BRIGHAM YOUNG UNIVERSITY

NEAL A. MAXWELL INSTITUTE

PROVO, UTAH

Daniel Becerra

The Book of Mormon: brief theological introductions series seeks Christ in scripture by combining intellectual rigor and the disciple's yearning for holiness. It answers Elder Neal A. Maxwell's call to explore the book's "divine architecture": "There is so much more in the Book of Mormon than we have yet discovered. The book's divine architecture and rich furnishings will increasingly unfold to our view, further qualifying it as '*a marvelous work and a wonder.*' (Isaiah 29:14) . . . All the rooms in this mansion need to be explored, whether by valued traditional scholars or by those at the cutting edge. Each plays a role, and one LDS scholar cannot say to the other, '*I have no need of thee.*'" [1] (1 Corinthians 12:21)

For some time, faithful scholars have explored the book's textual history, reception, historicity, literary quality, and more. This series focuses particularly on theology—the scholarly practice of exploring a scriptural text's implications and its lens on God's work in the world. Series volumes invite Latter-day Saints to discover additional dimensions of this treasured text but leave to prophets and apostles their unique role of declaring its definitive official doctrines. In this case, theology, as opposed to authoritative doctrine, relates to the original sense of the term as, literally, reasoned "God talk." The word also designates a well-developed academic field, but it is the more general sense of the term that most often applies here. By engaging each scriptural book's theology on its own terms, this series explores the spiritual and intellectual force of the ideas appearing in the Latter-day Saints' "keystone" scripture.

Series authors and editors possess specialized professional training that informs their work but, significantly, each takes Christ as theology's proper end because he is the proper end of all scripture and all reflection on it. We, too, "talk of Christ, we rejoice in Christ, we preach of Christ . . . that our children may know to what source they may look for a remission of their sins" (2 Nephi 25:26). Moreover, while experts in the modern disciplines of philosophy, theology, literature, and history, series authors and editors also work explicitly within the context of personal and institutional commitments both to Christian discipleship and to The Church of Jesus Christ of Latter-day Saints. These volumes are not official Church publications but can be best understood in light of these deep commitments. And because we acknowledge that scripture demands far more than intellectual experimentation, we call readers' attention to the processes of conversion and sanctification at play on virtually every scriptural page.

Individual series authors offer unique approaches but, taken together, they model a joint invitation to readers to engage scripture in their own way. No single approach to theology or scriptural interpretation commands preeminence in these volumes. No volume pretends to be the final word on theological reflection for its part of the Book of Mormon. Varied perspectives and methodologies are evident throughout. This is intentional. In addition, though we recognize love for the Book of Mormon is a "given" for most Latter-day Saint readers, we also share the conviction that, like the gospel of Jesus Christ itself, the Book of Mormon is inexhaustible.[2] These volumes invite readers to slow down and read scripture more thoughtfully and transformatively. Elder Maxwell cautioned against reading the Book of Mormon as "hurried tourists" who scarcely venture beyond "the entry hall."[3] To that end, we dedicate this series to his apostolic conviction that there is always more to learn from the Book of Mormon and much to be gained from our faithful search for Christ in its pages.

—The Editors

Contents

Introduction

The books of 3-4 Nephi are unique in the degree to which they focus on Jesus Christ and his teachings. Yet, when Mormon speaks about the Savior's visit to the Nephites, he remarks that "there cannot be written...even a hundredth part of the things which Jesus did truly teach" (3 Ne. 26:6; see also 3 Ne. 26:16; 27:23; 28:14). This statement suggests that the reader must approach these texts with the understanding that they never claim to be the full picture of or final word on Jesus Christ. Rather, they gesture beyond themselves, serving as tools whereby "greater things" may be revealed (3 Ne. 26:9). My purpose in this book, therefore, is not only to examine what 3-4 Nephi say but also to use them as a starting point in pursuit of Christ and Christlikeness.[1] I thus proceed with the assumption that the role of theology is not to draw a box around God but to search him out and, in so doing, to clear a path toward him. If I am successful in this work, you as the reader will come to encounter Christ and understand Christian discipleship in a more intimate way.

Given the brief nature of this book, I have been necessarily selective in the material that I address. Rather than moving through 3-4 Nephi chronologically, I structure the book thematically. This strategy allows me to draw out traditional theological themes like Christology (the nature of Christ), anthropology (human nature), and soteriology (the nature of salvation). Broadly speaking, theology is the study of the nature and work of the Godhead. It is a highly developed discipline in many Christian denominations, with a history spanning almost two thousand years. I periodically situate the teachings of 3–4 Nephi within this larger tradition of Christian thought. By demonstrating how the Book of Mormon is similar to and distinct from other theological writings, I hope to show how it might also be further illuminated by them. In this sense, this volume is not only about 3–4 Nephi but also about thinking with and beyond these texts in search of wisdom (see D&C 88:118).

Chapter 1 focuses on the language employed by Mormon in 3–4 Nephi to describe the Savior. I say "Mormon" because, while Nephi₁ 🖎 and his posterity recorded the history of the Nephites at this period in time (ca. 1–321 AD), it was Mormon who abridged their accounts and narrates the story to us (3 Ne. 5:10–12). In chapter 1, I examine the value and limitations of terms and images like *God, human, father,* and *mother* as bridges for understanding Christ's multifaceted nature. I suggest that coming unto Christ involves both knowing and unknowing him, meaning that, as disciples we must allow Christ to teach us as well as to defy our expectations. Chapter 2 turns to Mormon's understanding of human beings as they relate to God and to one another. I focus specifically on the ways in which Mormon maps a person's relationship with God onto every aspect of his or her identity: both the inner and the outer person. Chapter 3 is dedicated to the following questions: What does it mean to be like Christ? And what are some of the signs that the disciple is on the right path? I argue that Christlikeness finds its fullest expression in community, collaboration, and collectivity; this is a clear unifying theme of 3–4 Nephi. Chapter 4

🖎 Subscripts differentiate Nephi son of Helaman (Nephi₂) and Nephi son of Nephi (Nephi₃) from Nephi son of Lehi (Nephi₁) for quick reference. Other series volumes employ subscripts to similarly distinguish other Book of Mormon figures who share the same name: Mosiah, Helaman, Alma, and so forth.

examines the implications of Christian discipleship for public life. I identify three characteristics of the ideal society as Mormon portrays it: all things in common, equal access to great learning, and unity. It will become clear throughout these chapters that Christ is at the center of all theological thinking in 3–4 Nephi. Chapter 5 then offers some concluding reflections of the value of 3–4 Nephi for the disciple's pursuit of Christ and Christlikeness.

1

Christ

The coming of Christ to the Nephites is the most significant event in the Book of Mormon. It had been prophesied for generations. Signs and wonders heralded the day it would occur. Yet, when Christ descended from heaven, the Nephites did not recognize him. They "wist not what it meant, for they thought it was an angel that had appeared unto them" (3 Ne. 11:8). The prophecies of Christ up to this point in Nephite history present him as both human and divine, so what were the Nephites expecting? Someone less than an angel or more like a god? The Nephites did not know Christ as his followers in Palestine did. They never saw him hungry or thirsty. They never saw him tired or sick or bleeding. They had also never witnessed him calm the storm, heal the sick, and raise the dead. Like us, they relied primarily on teaching, preaching, and revelation to understand this being who was both God and human. And yet they still did not know quite what to expect.

Part of Mormon's project in 3–4 Nephi is to help his readers recognize Christ and consider what they might expect of their relationship with him. He is thus concerned not only with who Christ is but with who Christ is to us. By employing terms like *father* and *mother* in relation to the Savior, for example, Mormon invites the reader to consider the ways in which familial relations may serve as a paradigm for relating to Christ. At the same time, Mormon is aware of the limitations of such terms. That Christ can be both God and human, both male and female, both the Father and the Son, reminds us that the words used to describe him gesture toward, rather than completely circumscribe, his multifaceted nature. In 3–4 Nephi we are taught that Christ often transcends the boundaries we construct around him. This teaching should give the aspiring disciple cause to pause and reflect because the character of our discipleship emerges from our understanding of Christ. As I hope to demonstrate, there is utility in wrestling with the mysteries and complexities of the Savior's nature. The Christian theologian Origen of Alexandria (185–254 AD) once suggested that scripture expresses truth in complex and enigmatic ways because God wants to "exercise the understanding" of his followers.[1] In other words, God wants to teach us not just what to know but how to learn. This chapter attempts to more fully utilize the tools that 3–4 Nephi provides to learn about how Christ is like us, how he is different, and why it matters.

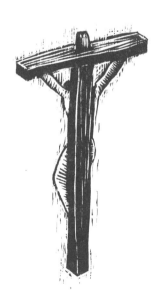

the wounded god

Jesus is referred to by more than thirty titles in 3–4 Nephi. One of the most common is "God," making Christ's divinity rather than his humanity a significant focus of these two books. Mormon's emphasis on Jesus's godhood is not unique. The Gospel of John, for example, begins with the author's declaration of "the Word," who was with God, is God, and is creator of all that exists (John 1:1). Other gospel authors equate Jesus, if only implicitly, with Jehovah of the Old Testament and the God of Abraham, Isaac, and Jacob (e.g., Matt. 1:23; 12:8). Jesus's divinity is theologically significant because it is what gives him the power to save: to bear the burden of human sin without collapsing under its weight and to lay down his life and take it up again. Jesus's divinity is what makes him different from us.

In the way that they emphasize this divine aspect of Jesus's nature, 3–4 Nephi are unique, however. Rather than appealing primarily to the Savior's miracles and power as proof of his divinity, as the gospel authors typically do, Mormon sees evidence of Christ's godhood in his wounded body. In other words, what makes Jesus human is also what makes him God. Before examining Mormon's portrayal of Christ in more detail, it may be helpful to briefly address how other theologians have understood the importance of the Savior's body. This contrast will help provide a better sense for how 3–4 Nephi are distinct, as well as for how they participate in a larger tradition of reflection about the nature of Christ, or what is commonly referred to as *Christology.*

Within the broader tradition of Christian theology, Jesus's body is significant for at least three reasons. It provides him perfect empathy for the human condition, allowing him to know experientially what we go through. It also enables him to accomplish the redemption of humankind. As the fourth-century theologian Gregory of Nazianzus (329–390 AD) taught, "what has not been assumed has not been healed," meaning that to save human bodies from the effects of sin and death, Christ had to take upon himself (i.e., assume) a human body.[2] He had to be like us in order to save us. Jesus's body also affirms the inherent goodness of our own bodies. In the ancient world it was not uncommon to view the physical matter that houses the human spirit as a kind of prison that must be escaped in pursuit of holiness. To some, however, Christ's body demonstrated that the human body was both good and central to God's plan for humankind. In these instances, Jesus's body hearkens to his humanity and elevates ours.

By way of contrast, in 3–4 Nephi, Christ's body, and more specifically his wounds, primarily reflect his divinity. Mormon records in vivid detail how Jesus descended from heaven in light and glory, "showing his body" to the Nephites and inviting them to "thrust [their] hands into [his] side, and...feel the prints of the nails in [his] hands and in [his] feet" (3 Ne. 10:19; 11:14). The purpose of Christ showing his body, Mormon tells us, was that the people might "know of a surety and...bear record" that the man before them was in fact "the God of Israel, and the God of the whole earth...slain for the sins of the world...he, of whom it was written by the prophets, that should come" (3 Ne. 11:14–15). Thus, even more explicitly than in the Gospel of John (John 20:20–29), Jesus's wounded body serves as a witness to his godhood and his prophesied atonement. It is what sets him apart from the rest of the human family as the Savior and God of the earth. Understanding this, the Nephites then cry out, "Hosanna! Blessed be the name of the Most High God! And they did fall down at the feet of Jesus, and did worship him" (3 Ne. 11:17).

It is significant that Christ chooses the only physical imperfections on his resurrected body to testify of his perfection. Why choose marks of human frailty to convince others of divine power? Or why evoke signs of death to prove that you are the "life of the world" (3 Ne. 11:11)? After all, earlier Nephite tradition about the resurrected body emphasized its wholeness, that "even a hair of the head shall not be lost; but all things shall be restored to their proper and perfect frame" (Alma 40:23). At the very least, his wounded body would have been a reminder to the Nephites that, while a God, Jesus was very much like them. By blurring the lines between humanity and divinity, between creator and creation, Christ may have taught the people something of their own potential, that what made them human was not incompatible with godliness. And perhaps this was the point. The Nephites were absent during the Savior's mortal ministry and thus had fewer points of reference for understanding what made him like and unlike them. By presenting himself as a wounded God, Christ provided the Nephites with a bridge for understanding his multifaceted nature, as well as their own.

Moreover, having recently endured the darkness and devastation associated with the Savior's death, the Nephites likely had their own scars, still aching and reminding them of the emotional and physical trauma they had just experienced. Mormon tells us that prior to Christ's appearance there were "deaths and destructions by fire, and by smoke, and by tempests, and by whirlwinds, and by the opening of the earth" and that "the mourning, and the weeping, and the wailing" of those who survived could be heard in the darkness (3 Ne. 10:10, 14). These wounded people now stood before a wounded God. In Christ's maimed hands and feet, the Nephites may have seen themselves. Or maybe they remembered the "railing and persecution and all manner of afflictions" that they had suffered on Christ's behalf in the years prior, when they were awaiting his coming (3 Ne. 6:13; see also 3 Ne. 1:13). And then, in this moment, perhaps they were reminded of how Christ had similarly suffered on their behalf during this time.

Throughout 3–4 Nephi, Mormon's portrayal of Christ is intended to build such bridges of understanding. He wants the reader not just to know about Christ but to know him personally. He thus employs language and imagery that prompt reflection and introspection and that invite readers to use their own life experiences as tools for coming unto Christ, one of the most prominent themes in these two books (3 Ne. 9:13; 10:6; 12:20; 21:6; 24:7; 27:20; 30:2). At the same time, by drawing upon such a rich variety of descriptive terms and titles, Mormon resists the tendency to put constraints on Christ. In so doing, he prompts readers to question their assumptions and to reevaluate their expectations regarding the Savior.

christ as father

Another example of Mormon building bridges of understanding may be seen in his portrayal of Christ as father. There is a discernible emphasis on Jesus's role as father in 3–4 Nephi, as well as throughout the large plates, which are also the product of Mormon's editorial hand. Sometimes Mormon merely emphasizes the similarities between Jesus and God "the Father": that they share the same will, perfection, and doctrine, for example (3 Ne. 9:15; 11:11, 27, 32; 12:48; 19:23). At other times, he explicitly refers to Jesus by the title "father," saying that he is the "Father of heaven and earth," "the very Eternal Father," and "both the Father and the Son" (3 Ne. 1:14; Mosiah 3:8; 15:1–5; Alma 11:39; Hel. 14:12; Ether 4:7). Mormon appears to communicate something very specific in these latter passages. As other scholars have observed, in the Book of Mormon Christ's paternity hearkens to his role as the creator of the world and as Israel's guardian, to his conception by God's power, and to the fact that he spiritually begets his disciples, who take upon themselves his name and characteristics.[3] I suggest, however, that these characterizations do not exhaust the relevance of Christ's fatherhood for the reader. The title "father" has additional potential for helping disciples know and come unto Christ.

Were one to pose the question, How is Christ a father?, some responses might relate to how he loves, guides, and protects his followers, as well as to how he sacrifices, provides, and wants what is best for them. Such responses would be completely consistent with Mormon's portrayal of Christ in 3–4 Nephi. In fact, these books are unique in the degree that they portray Jesus interacting with the Nephites in what many might consider "fatherly" ways. 🖝 For example, he is physically present among them (3 Ne. 11–26). He is patient with their imperfections and tailors his teaching to their needs and intellectual abilities (3 Ne. 17:2–3, 8). He weeps for their failures and takes joy in their successes (3 Ne. 17:14, 20). He is filled with compassion toward them and takes time to bless them individually (3 Ne. 17:6–21). And he clearly wants to remain with them even though he is needed elsewhere (3 Ne. 17:5–6).

While such a portrayal of Christ may also reflect the reader's own positive experiences with the Savior, it does not fully encompass the concept of "father" as a bridge for understanding Jesus's nature. For instance, when we reflect on Christ's paternity, we may imagine what a perfect father would be like, and then ask ourselves, How is Christ like that to his disciples? This is not an incorrect way to understand our relationship with the Savior. But what if one were to similarly consider what imperfect

🖝 These traits could certainly also be predicated to mothers.

fathers might also reveal about the disciple's relationship with the Savior? By *imperfect* I do not mean abusive or cruel, but imperfect within the normal bounds of human imperfection. What if we were to take into account all of the fallibility and failures of real fathers, and all of our complex and sometimes strained relationships with them, and ask, How might these relationships serve as a tool for knowing and coming to Christ?

It would be theologically problematic to say that Christ is imperfect in the same way that earthly fathers are, but our relationship with imperfect fathers can provide tools for navigating those times in which our relationship with Christ fails to live up to our expectations. The reality of mortality is that disciples will not always feel close to Christ, and they will not always feel Christ close to them. Just as in relationships with imperfect fathers, sometimes there will be failed expectations, and there is power in accepting and expecting this. Perhaps most importantly, it may help us to faithfully endure periods of distance from the Savior, knowing that they are a part of the plan, rather than evidence of its or our inadequacies.

At such times, we might imagine Christ saying to us, for example: "Expect that sometimes you will become mad, frustrated, and impatient with me. Expect that sometimes you will feel like I am distant or too busy for you. This is entirely normal. Sometimes it may seem like I don't 'get you' or that I don't understand the urgency of your concerns and questions. Periodically you'll become tired of me or want nothing to do with me. You may feel like you need just a little time, a little space. This too is normal. Expect that sometimes you may feel embarrassed by me, or afraid to acknowledge me in public. Expect to not see all the ways that I care for and sustain you, and for this to sometimes affect our relationship negatively. You may even feel like I have forsaken you; I felt this way with my father too" (see Mark 15:34; Matt. 27:46).

More so than in any other book in the Book of Mormon, in 3 Nephi Christ is present among his people; they see him, they hear him, and they feel him. His absence, however, is felt just as keenly, especially by his disciples; it creates doubt, disbelief, fear, and sadness in them. Mormon records that at least some of these feelings were due to the faithful's frustrated expectations regarding how and when Christ would manifest himself to them. In some cases, the faithful thought he would arrive sooner than he did and stay longer than he was able (3 Ne. 1:7–10; 2:1; 8:4; 17:5). When this did not occur, they became "very sorrowful" and "began to disbelieve all which they had heard and seen" regarding him (3 Ne. 1:7; 2:1). In other cases, the Savior was present among them in spirit, but the faithful "knew it not," or he spoke to his people and "they understood it not" (3 Ne. 9:20; 11:4). What then should the disciple expect of Christ?

The sacramental promise of Christ's continual presence, whether personally or in spirit, is not made in 3–4 Nephi. Whereas Moroni records that persons are to covenant to "always remember him [Christ]...that they may *always* have his Spirit to be with them," Christ in 3 Nephi says, "if ye do always remember me ye shall have my Spirit to be with you" (Moro. 4:3, italics added; 3 Ne. 18:7). While subtle, Christ's omission of the second *always* in this promise may be theologically significant because it implies that the absence of the Holy Spirit does not necessarily connote a lapse in discipleship; it does not mean that we have failed to "remember" Christ, with all that entails.

In seeking to reconcile his desire for the Spirit with the reality of his experience, the fourth-century

Christian monk Ammonas provides a helpful way to think about the Spirit's presence and absence as it relates to discipleship. He writes:

> In the beginning of spiritual life, the Holy Spirit gives people joy when He sees their hearts becoming pure. But after the Spirit has given them joy and sweetness, He then departs and leaves them. This is a sign of His activity and happens with every soul that seeks and fears God. He departs and keeps his distance until He knows whether they will go on seeking Him or not.... If He sees that they are asking in uprightness from their whole heart and are denying all their own self-will, God in his grace will give them greater joy than the first, and establish them more firmly. This is a sign that He gives to every soul that seeks God.[4]

According to Ammonas, the Spirit's absence is not always punitive; sometimes it is pedagogical, an invitation to the disciple to reach out to God, and a means for a Father to bless his children. Or put a slightly different way, Christ's departure, though painful, always anticipates his return. One sees a similar principle articulated in 3 Nephi. Mormon tells us that Christ periodically withdraws and withholds from his people in order to "try their faith" or to allow them time to "ponder" and "prepare" themselves for his return (3 Ne. 17:3; 26:9). In such cases, the cavity quarried by Christ's absence creates more space for his indwelling; it allows him to bless his followers with "greater things" (3 Ne. 26:9). And in the same way that eyes in darkness are most sensitive to light, so periods of distance from the Savior help his people to better discern, know, and appreciate him.

christ as mother

Feminine imagery also serves in 3–4 Nephi as a bridge to understanding Christ's nature. Mormon is not unique in his portrayal of deity as a female figure. Numerous biblical authors compare God or Christ to a mother who comforts her child, a mother bear, a mother eagle, a mother hen, a nursing mother, a woman in labor, and a woman looking for a lost coin (Deut. 32:11–12; Hosea 13:8; Isa. 42:14; 49:15; 66:13; Ps. 131:2; Matt. 23:37; Luke 15:8–10). As may be seen from these examples, when God and Christ are described using feminine imagery, they are typically portrayed not only as women but also as mothers. Mormon's description of Christ mirrors most closely the Gospel of Matthew, in which the Savior is described as a mother hen who gathers her chicks. Mormon's account, however, is also distinct from Matthew's, and that distinction may serve to deepen the reader's understanding of Christ as a maternal figure.

Matthew 23:37 records Jesus mourning the wickedness of Jerusalem. Following his rebuke of the scribes and pharisees, Christ says, "O Jerusalem, Jerusalem, thou that killest the prophets, and stonest them which are sent unto thee, how often would I have gathered thy children together, even as a hen gathereth her chickens under her wings, and ye would not!" Christ's lament in 3 Nephi is similar but not the same. Mormon records that, following the three-day period of death and destruction, "there was silence in all the land for the space of many hours. And it came to pass that there came a voice again unto the people, and all the people did hear" (3 Ne. 10:2–3). Christ compares himself to a mother hen, saying:

> O ye people of these great cities which have fallen, who are descendants of Jacob, yea, who

16

are of the house of Israel, how oft have I gathered you as a hen gathereth her chickens under
her wings, and have nourished you.

And again, how oft would I have gathered you as
a hen gathereth her chickens under her wings,
yea, O ye people of the house of Israel, who
have fallen; yea, O ye people of the house of
Israel ... ye that have fallen; yea, how oft would I
have gathered you as a hen gathereth her chickens, and ye would not.

O ye house of Israel whom I have spared, how
oft will I gather you as a hen gathereth her chickens under her wings, if ye will repent and return
unto me with full purpose of heart. (3 Ne. 10:4–6)

How might this more extended lament contribute to
the reader's understanding of Christ?

At the very least, it conveys the depth of the Savior's
love, sadness, and unwavering commitment to Israel.[5]
The four-fold repetition of the "how oft" statements,
for example, rhetorically portrays Christ as an impas-
sioned mother, intervening to try to help her wayward
child. As if sitting across the table from the child, she
recounts her previous efforts to assist him, saying,
"How oft have I gathered you ... and have nourished
you." She is not posing a question; she is making a
statement. Then, with slightly distinct phrasing, she
says, "How oft *would* I have gathered you." Again, this
is not a question but an assertion of her past willingness to help her child. Feeling perhaps heartbro-
ken, helpless, and betrayed, she then adds, "How oft
would I have gathered you ... *and ye would not*." Here
it becomes clear that the child's intransigence is what
prevents the mother from helping. Notwithstanding

this, her love is constant, not predicated upon recip-rocation, and she declares her unwavering commit-ment saying, "How oft *will* I gather you." Cumulatively, Christ says, in effect: "I have done everything I could," "I would do more if you let me," and "I will continue to do everything I can." For Mormon, Christ's maternity is reflected at least in the consistency of his love: that he has, does, would, and will continue to extend his hand to Israel.

Mormon is not the only Book of Mormon author to teach about Christ using feminine imagery. In 1 Nephi, Nephi₁ reproduces the messianic language of Isaiah 49:15–16, writing, "Can a woman forget her sucking child, that she should not have compassion on the son of her womb? Yea, they may forget, yet will I not forget thee.... Behold, I have graven thee upon the palms of my hands" (1 Ne. 21:15–16). In this passage, the wounds of Christ's crucifixion are analogous to a nursing moth-er's engorged breasts; they are a persistent, embodied reminder of her children and their needs. Christ can-not but remember the children of Israel; it pains him not to nourish them. At the same time, by also stating that mothers "may forget [their children], yet will I not forget thee" (1 Ne. 21:15), Christ gestures toward what we perhaps cannot yet fully understand. He invites us to reach beyond all the love we know, the purest we can muster, the deepest we have experienced, and there to find him. Then we will know how he feels toward us. It is not just that he loves us; it is that he knows no other way. He cannot help but love; he needs to love. Here, as in 3 Nephi, feminine imagery serves as a bridge to understanding Christ's nature.

The image of the feminine Christ also invites the disciple to see Christ in women, invites women to see Christ in themselves, and encourages reflection on the ways in which womanhood is akin to and anticipates godhood. The metaphor of motherhood similarly elevates women and provides more intimate knowledge of the Savior. In the case of 1 Nephi 21, the metaphor is perhaps most fully intelligible to women who have breastfed children, partly because maternity is embodied in such mothers in a way that lacks parallel for other people. For example, as a man, I do not fully understand what it is like to physically and involuntarily ache to nourish another human being. Consequently, the utility of the image of a nursing mother for helping me comprehend Christ's commitment to Israel is limited. I can certainly extrapolate based on my own experiences with love for my children and others, but I still lack the foundational knowledge upon which the metaphor is based. The metaphor of motherhood in 3 Nephi, on the other hand, is distinct. Because it does not explicitly rely on embodied aspects of maternity as a referent, it encourages the reader to consider other ways in which motherhood is experienced, such as by mothers who have not physically borne or nursed children. It also assumes the equal value of such experiences for coming to know the Savior. Mormon thus opens a window to Christ's soul for all kinds of mothers and demonstrates that being a mother can become a way to see with Christ's eyes, feel with his heart, and understand with his mind.

the ideal of christlikeness
By this point it should be clear that Mormon provides the reader with numerous bridges to understanding the Savior's multifaceted nature. While these bridges lead to greater knowledge of Christ, they also direct disciples toward a fuller understanding of themselves and their potential. This is because the heart of discipleship is the imitation of Christ; Christ and the disciple must reflect each other (3 Ne. 18:24). It is abundantly

clear in 3–4 Nephi that Jesus wants his disciples to be like him. He not only commands them to be "even as I am" in the present but promises them a future reward in which they "shall be even as I am" (3 Ne. 12:48; 27:27; 28:10). Christlikeness is thus the beginning and the end of discipleship (3 Ne. 9:18).

What then does it mean to be like Christ? One way to answer this question would be in general terms. At the very least, Christlikeness implies moral and physical perfection (3 Ne. 12:48), meaning the possession of all moral attributes in their fullness and a resurrected body. I will address the nature of perfection in more detail in chapter 3. Another way to approach the question would be to examine how Christ describes himself in 3–4 Nephi. In doing so, however, the reader is immediately confronted with the fact that the Savior frequently "overlaps" with other persons, making it difficult to discern where he ends and another person or being begins. To aid our understanding of the theological significance of this "overlapping," I will provide some examples of what I mean.

Consider the following statements made by Jesus about himself:

"I come . . . to do the will, both of the Father and of the Son—of the Father because of me, and of the Son because of my flesh" (3 Ne. 1:14)

"I am in the Father, and the Father in me" (3 Ne. 9:15)

"The Father, and the Son, and the Holy Ghost are one; and I am in the Father, and the Father in me, and the Father and I are one" (3 Ne. 11:27)

"The Father, and I, and the Holy Ghost are one"
   (3 Ne. 11:36)

"Be perfect even as I, or your Father who is in
   heaven is perfect" (3 Ne. 12:48)

"I am even as the Father; and the Father and I are one"
   (3 Ne. 28:10)

In each of these passages, Christ is not uniquely himself. He is either *like*, or *one with*, or *in* other members of the Godhead. This raises the question, If Christ overlaps with others, what does it mean for the disciple to be like Christ? Or, put another way, How is Christ's relational nature to be reflected in the life of the disciple?

Some Christian theologians have insightfully seen Christ's relationality as a blueprint for ideal human relations both with God and with one another.[6] Gregory of Nazianzus, for example, taught that the unity, love, and peace that characterize the Father, Son, and Holy Spirit's relationship should be reflected in our dealings with one another. We are to become "one" as they are one, "same in heart and in honor…with, not against, one another" and "unified completely in the Spirit."[7] Christ expresses this same sentiment in 3 Nephi, praying to be "in" his disciples "as thou, Father, art in me, that we may be one" (3 Ne. 19:23; cf. John 17:21). In this passage, "oneness" and "in-ness" are not states of existence that are possible only for the Godhead. Christ also intends these states to characterize the disciple's relationship with deity and with one another.

Because Christ cannot be fully understood independent of his relation to others, discipleship must also be understood in relational terms. As I hope to demonstrate in the following chapters, Christlikeness finds its fullest expression in community, collaboration, and collectivity. And disciples may be seen to reflect the Savior's relational nature in various ways, at all stages of their journey of discipleship, and in multiple aspects of their identity. Before addressing what makes a human like Christ, however, it will be helpful to first explore in more detail what makes a human a human.

2

Humankind

Mormon's discussion of human nature in 3–4 Nephi reveals some of the complexities and paradoxes of our existence. He demonstrates that humans are both fundamentally flawed and endowed with divinity. Our identity both encompasses and transcends the boundaries of our individual bodies, meaning that while each of us are uniquely ourselves, disciples of Christ are also expected to be "one" with each other and with God (3 Ne. 19:23). Thus, like Christ, we are to "overlap" with one another. Additionally, Mormon teaches that God is the father of all humankind but that not all humans are necessarily his children. He shows that human agency is both vitally important and utterly insufficient for bridging the gap between one's nature and one's destiny. In more traditional theological language, these subjects comprise what may be considered Mormon's "theological anthropology."

Understanding human nature is valuable because it provides a foundation for understanding human potential. Who we are determines who we can become, how we get there, and what we might expect along the way (all of which will be addressed in the following pages). Because all humans bear the image of our creator, understanding ourselves may also contribute to our knowledge of and relationship with God and one another. Mormon's discussion of the various facets of human nature is neither systematic nor limited to 3–4 Nephi. For this reason, I make some effort to situate Mormon's thinking within the context of his other writings. Elsewhere in the large plates, his views on agency and the effects of the fall, for instance, inform his discussion in 3–4 Nephi of what it means to be a child of God. Statements regarding the relationship of skin color and morality similarly appear throughout the large plates and play a significant theological role in 3–4 Nephi. In this sense, Mormon periodically sows seeds of theological principles elsewhere in the Book of Mormon, which then come to bear fruit in 3–4 Nephi.

the inner person

To begin, we might ask what a person is on the most basic level and how this understanding of human nature can point us to Christ. Mormon depicts human beings as comprised of parts and faculties. Throughout the large plates, the parts of a person that he refers to are the heart, mind, soul, spirit, and body/flesh (two terms that are often used synonymously). ☞ Each part, in turn, possesses at least one of the following faculties: ① cognition: the capacity for thinking, imagining, perceiving, deliberating, understanding, believing, knowing, and recollection; ② emotion: the capacity for feeling; and ③ volition: the capacity for desiring, intending, choosing, ardor, and appetite. Mormon, of course, does not use these three technical terms, but I employ them here as a helpful way to categorize the many terms he does use. FIGURE 1 represents each part of the human being and its attendant faculties as Mormon understands them.¹

Christ's relationality is reflected in the mechanics of how we function as humans. First, Mormon does not restrict individual faculties to a single part of the human being. For example, in one passage he writes that the Nephites "did understand in their hearts" the

☞ Some of these terms are fluid. For example, *soul* is sometimes used to refer to the whole human person, such as in 3 Nephi 5:1, 20; 17:25. Also, *soul* and *spirit* both periodically appear to be shorthand for the noncorporeal self (e.g., 1 Ne. 15:31; 19:7, 20; 2 Ne. 9:12; Alma 36:15).

Parts	Faculties	Example scripture references
Heart	Cognition	3 Ne. 1:22; 17:17; 19:33
	Emotion	3 Ne. 1:10; 4:33
	Volition	4 Ne. 1:15; 3 Ne. 5:5; 12:24,28
Mind	Cognition	3 Ne. 2:1; 17:3
	Emotion	Alma 15:3; 30:53; 42:1
	Volition	Mosiah 4:13; 7:33; Alma 35:5–6
Soul	Emotion	3 Ne. 17:17; Hel. 7:8–9;
	Volition	Alma 5:43; 34:26
	Cognition	Alma 14:6; Morm. 9:3
Spirit	Emotion	3 Ne. 9:20; 12:19; 22:6
Flesh	Volition	Mosiah 16:12

FIGURE 1 Parts and faculties of the human being

words of Jesus; here the heart is responsible for the cognitive act of understanding (3 Ne. 19:33). Elsewhere, however, he portrays belief (also a form of cognition) as the work of the mind (3 Ne. 2:1; 7:16). In these instances, the heart and mind remain distinct but share responsibilities. Christ's description of the Godhead in 3 Nephi mirrors Mormon's understanding of human nature, thereby gesturing toward one way in which humans reflect Christ. Referring specifically to the Godhead's shared work of bearing witness, Jesus teaches, "I bear record of the Father, and the Father beareth record of me, and the Holy Ghost beareth record of the Father and me" (3 Ne. 11:32; see also verses 35–36). In this passage, the work of bearing witness is distributed to all members of the Godhead. By drawing a parallel between the most fundamental aspects of human identity on the one hand and divine operations on the other, Christ teaches us that by thoughtfully looking inward, the disciple may also be directed upward toward a fuller understanding of deity.

Mormon also periodically describes the individual parts of the human being as having the potential to be shared by multiple persons simultaneously, albeit figuratively. The fullest description of what this looks like occurs in 3 Nephi, but statements also appear elsewhere. For example, Mormon writes in Mosiah that the Nephites must aspire to have their "hearts knit together" (Mosiah 18:21–22). Nephi$_1$ employs similar language, saying that disciples should strive to share "one mind" and "one heart" (2 Ne. 1:21). It is not until 3 Nephi, however, that Jesus prays for his people to "be one" with him and God (3 Ne. 19:23, 29; cf. John 17:21). Here, two things become apparent: ① the ideal of oneness is not to be limited to human relations, and ② Christ's relationality with the Godhead provides a model of unity toward which humans are to strive.

This ideal of oneness has powerful implications. Perhaps most significantly, it suggests that God's goal for humankind cannot be understood strictly with respect to an individual in isolation. In much the same way that Paul views the faithful as collectively constituting the body of Christ (1 Cor. 12:12), so Mormon imagines Christian identity as relational: numerous persons intersecting, or "overlapping," with individual bodies but not confined by their boundaries. This overlapping, of course, is not to be taken literally, but it does hearken to the prevalent notion in 3–4 Nephi that Christian discipleship is founded upon unity, other-centeredness, and outward-orientation.

fallen humanity

Although some aspects of human nature may be understood to point the disciple to Christ, others point toward the ways in which we are different from him. Throughout the large plates, Mormon expresses the view that human nature, while retaining some semblance of divinity and capacity for goodness, is also severely corrupted. His understanding of fallen humanity in turn informs his discussion in 3–4 Nephi of what it means to be a "child of God." In this sense, Mormon articulates a theological principle elsewhere in the large plates that provides a foundation for understanding his teachings in 3–4 Nephi. Along the way, he also demonstrates that knowing what makes us different from God helps us to better understand what is required of us to become like him.

Mormon teaches that after the fall of Adam and Eve, men and women became enemies to God, "carnal," "sensual," "devilish," "lost," worthless, nothing, and spiritually dead (Mosiah 3:19; 4:5; 16:3–5; Alma 42:9–10; Hel. 12:7). Thus, by virtue of being born, every human being exists in "a state of nature"—sometimes referred to as the "natural man"—that is "contrary to the nature of God" (Alma 41:11). This is not to say that the fall was not a step forward for human progression. It is merely to say that it was also a step down. Being mortal, all of us find ourselves continually subject to temptation, enticed by sin, and prone to err. As Elder Bednar has taught, "The very elements out of which our bodies were created are by nature fallen and ever subject to the pull of sin."[2] Mormon argues that another consequence of humanity's fallenness is that human agency by itself is utterly insufficient for altering our fallen identity. He explains that "since man had fallen he could not merit anything of himself," suggesting, at least, that all of our efforts to be righteous are not what ultimately save us (Alma 22:14).

However, Mormon simultaneously portrays fallenness as a kind of choice, something that one voluntarily "persists in" by electing "the ways of sin and rebellion against God" (Mosiah 16:5). In this sense, Mormon elevates the importance of human agency in attaining salvation. He frames a person's "carnal nature" and "fallen state" as matters of the will, or as states of being that one might opt out of, in addition to intrinsic human attributes (Mosiah 16:5). He also characterizes fallen persons as those who "never called upon the Lord while the arms of mercy were extended towards them" and who "would not depart" from their iniquities (Mosiah 16:2–5, 12). Put simply, *fallenness* in Mormon's thought comprises both the involuntary orientation toward sin inherent in mortality and the willful commission of it. The theological significance of this somewhat paradoxical presentation lies in the implication that humans, while fallen, retain some power and responsibility to improve their situation and transform their lives.

Finally, in contrast to some other Christian thinkers, Mormon believes that human fallenness does not make us worthy of punishment. Thus, 3–4 Nephi stand at odds with the doctrine of "original sin" championed by the Christian theologian Augustine (354–430 AD). According to Augustine, fallen humans are guilty of damnation solely by virtue of being born. Mormon, however, teaches that while humanity experiences the negative effects of Adam and Eve's choices, we are born blameless and held accountable only for the improper exercise of our own will. He thus explains that those "who have died not knowing the will of God concerning them, or who have ignorantly sinned" are not subject to penalties for sin (Mosiah 3:11; see also Mosiah 3:18; Moro. 8:5–20). What then does Mormon's understanding of fallenness and agency have to do with the teaching in 3–4 Nephi that we are children of God?

divine humanity

The notion that human beings are inherently God's off-spring is not prevalent in the Book of Mormon. Instead, familial kinship with the divine is most often something that is attained, not assumed. Accordingly, while Mormon refers to both God and Jesus as the father and creator of humankind, the phrases "sons of God," "children of God," "children of your Father," and "children of Christ" are reserved for only those who through their own faithfulness and Christ's intercession have had this status bestowed upon them (3 Ne. 9:17; 12:9, 45; 4 Ne. 1:17, 39; see also Mosiah 5:7; 18:22; Alma 6:6; 30:42; Moro. 7:26, 48). ☞

Mormon's understanding of fallen human nature described elsewhere in the large plates explains why in 3–4 Nephi humans are not always portrayed as children of God by default: although born sinless, we are involuntarily oriented toward sin (i.e., enticed by it and prone to commit it). His understanding of human agency provides a theological foundation for the notion that kinship with God is a choice: we must opt out of our fallenness in order to be adopted by God. For instance, echoing similar statements found in the New Testament, Christ says in 3 Nephi, "as many as have received me, to them have I given to become the sons of God; and even so will I to as many as shall believe on my name" (3 Ne. 9:17; cf. Rom. 8:14–17; John 1:12). Elsewhere in scripture, making peace with, loving, blessing, praying for, and doing good to others is what qualifies one to be a child of God (3 Ne. 12:9, 44–45; cf. Matt. 5:44–45). In 4 Nephi, Mormon uses the phrase "children of God" to distinguish disciples from those who willfully "rebel against the gospel of Christ" (4 Ne. 1:38–39). In these passages,

☞ At times it is not explicit that the term *child(ren)* is used to refer specifically to the faithful. However, this seems to be the case from context. See 1 Nephi 11:17; 17:36; 22:25; 2 Nephi 6:12; Alma 13:1.

30

kinship with deity is moral and covenantal, not an inherent aspect of human identity. ☞

Traditionally in Christian theology, discussions of humankind's relationship to God reference Genesis 1:26–27, in which humans are said to be created in God's "image" and "likeness." Theologians commonly understand God's image/likeness to comprise shared human and divine attributes like rationality, virtue, creativity, sovereignty, and freedom, all of which may augment as humans spiritually mature. In Latter-day Saint thought, this scriptural passage is sometimes understood as a reference to the anthropomorphic form of God's body, which mirrors our own. However, 3–4 Nephi make no allusion to Genesis, and explicit mention of God's image/likeness in humankind is entirely absent. This is not to say that Mormon believed humanity lacks the imprint of its maker; he certainly alludes to Genesis 1:26–27 elsewhere in the large plates (e.g., Mosiah 7:27; Alma 5:14, 19; 18:34; 22:12). Rather, in 3–4 Nephi he is selective in his discussion in that he is primarily concerned with the role of human agency in establishing kinship with God and not with the seed of divinity already present within us. His understanding of human nature, therefore, begins with our fallenness, and not with our goodness.

Mormon's emphasis on conditional kinship represents a subtle yet important distinction from the modern Church's emphasis on all humanity being intrinsically children of God. As "The Family: A Proclamation to the World" states, "All human beings—male and female—are created in the image of God. Each is a beloved spirit son or daughter of heavenly parents." This difference between Mormon's understanding and the modern Church's proclamation raises the question,

☞ Moroni also suggests as much in Moroni 7:48. The phrase "child(ren) of the devil" in the Book of Mormon functions similarly.

What is the utility of understanding one's relationship to deity in these different ways? For example, if we were to contemplate the phrase "I am a child of God," how might that affect us differently than contemplating the question "Am I a child of God?" Internalizing the notion that God is father to all encourages us to see each other as equals, as gods in embryo, and as dear to deity. This line of teaching is certainly present in the Book of Mormon (3 Ne. 14:7–11; see also Jacob 2:21; Alma 39:17; Moro. 8:12). It also reminds us that, while fallen creatures, we cannot escape our potential for goodness; it is in our spiritual genes. The assumption of unconditional kinship, therefore, at the very least elevates human nature and provides humans with confidence that God loves them and is mindful of their needs.

Internalizing the notion that God is father only to the faithful, on the other hand, may have different positive effects. The knowledge that kinship is bestowed and transitory creates productive uneasiness in the soul by calling into question whether who we currently are is who we should be. It is an invitation to self-evaluation, to gaze upon the gulf separating the soul's state and the soul's objective in all its terrifying profundity. This realization of our distance from God may in turn serve to bring us closer to one another. When we fail to honestly acknowledge our own sins and weaknesses, we can prevent ourselves from using them as sources of understanding, empathy, and compassion. We render ourselves incapable of offering real service to the many who similarly suffer as a result of the fallen human condition. As one Catholic priest observed, "If you're a stranger to your own wound, then you're gonna be tempted to despise the wounded."[3] In this sense, human imperfections can help us to know, love, and serve God and one another. It is perhaps for this reason that Mormon chooses to emphasize human fallenness and the importance of agency in 3–4 Nephi. He does not appear to view our flawed nature and inherent divinity as mutually incompatible, but he focuses on the former to help readers better know how to nourish the latter in themselves and one another.

Mormon's understanding of human fallenness and conditional kinship with God also presents a challenge to the valuation placed on "authenticity" in modern society.[4] By authenticity, I am not referring to the laudable traits of integrity, honesty, and sincerity, all of which Christ encourages in 3 Nephi (e.g., 3 Ne. 13:1–7, 16–18).[5] Rather, I refer to the assumption that what is "natural" (e.g., our inherent inclinations and desires) should also be normative, that the highest good is "allegiance to one's internal feelings and impulses," independent of external standards of conduct or character.[6] Blurring the line between what we want to do and what we ought to do risks neglecting what is best in order to pursue what is most pleasurable or convenient. This is not to suggest that God does not want people to be themselves. Rather, Mormon would argue that being true to ourselves is a viable principle for self-governance only when we are living "in Christ" (4 Ne. 1:23). Authenticity in this sense is relational, not individualistic. It is a partnership: the authentic self must reflect the indwelling Christ; or, as Christ teaches the Nephites, "hold up your light that it may shine unto the world. Behold I am the light which ye shall hold up" (3 Ne. 18:24).

The spiritual renovation of his readers is clearly part of Mormon's project in 3–4 Nephi. For this reason, his discussion of human-divine kinship focuses on agency. It is peppered with exhortations to love, bless, pray, and do good. And, significantly, these commands were not issued to the wicked but to the "more righteous part of the people" (3 Ne. 10:12), with the purpose of enabling them to become children of God

(3 Ne. 12:44–45). Jesus, therefore, may be seen to invite all those who view themselves as righteous to thoughtfully consider the question, Am I a child of God?

the outer person

Another aspect of the human identity that is addressed in 3–4 Nephi is physical appearance (i.e., the "outer person"), which Mormon frequently correlates to one's relationship with God and others. This occurs primarily through his discussions of skin color. The argument may be made that such passages do not pair well with our modern sensibilities. I would suggest, however, that merely ignoring them is just as imprudent as focusing on nothing else but them. As I hope to demonstrate, Mormon's discussion of the more visible aspects of human identity ultimately points the reader toward their insignificance. As previously intimated, what Christ offers in 3–4 Nephi is a new form of kinship, one not predicated upon race and genealogy but upon covenant and adoption.

Morality and complexion are linked from the very beginning of the Book of Mormon. In 2 Nephi 5:21, Nephi$_1$ writes that the Lord caused "a skin of blackness" to come upon his rebellious brothers, as if to mirror their wickedness epidermally (cf. 1 Ne. 12:23). He explains: "as they were white, and exceedingly fair and delightsome," they now "had become like unto a flint" (2 Ne. 5:21). Mormon would later describe the consequences of this change on their posterity in the following way: "The skins of the Lamanites were dark, according to the mark which was set upon their fathers, which was a curse upon them because of their transgression and their rebellion against their brethren, who consisted of Nephi, Jacob, and Joseph, and Sam, who were just and holy men" (Alma 3:6). Darkness of skin in the Book of Mormon, therefore, comes to be associated with a people who are "loathsome," "full of mischief and subtlety," "idle," filthy, hated, reviled, and a "scourge" to God's people (1 Ne. 12:23; 2 Ne. 5:22–25; Jacob 3:5, 9; Morm. 5:15).

Perhaps in response to the problematic implications and damaging effects of such a portrayal on persons of color,[7] some modern interpreters have sought to distinguish between the "curse" and the "mark" spoken of by Mormon by arguing that the curse was in fact separation from the Lord and his people while the mark was darker skin.[8] Others have suggested that dark skin is merely a metaphor, a literary symbol for the Lamanites' spiritual depravity, or that it is a remnant of nineteenth-century racist sentiments.[9] According to these interpretations, darkness of skin is not inherently bad but is a sign of badness only in this particular instance. Still others have suggested that the Lamanites' dark skins refer to animal hides, which they donned as a kind of tribal vestment.[10] This latter argument, however, seems unlikely given Mormon's insinuation that dark skin was passed on through procreation (Alma 3:9; see also 2 Ne. 5:22–25).[11]

In the same way that the darkening of skin is correlated to wickedness in 3–4 Nephi, so the whitening of skin is associated with righteousness, a phenomenon unique to Mormon's writings. Mormon records that "those Lamanites who had united with the Nephites were numbered among the Nephites; And their curse was taken from them, and their skin became white like unto the Nephites; And their young men and their daughters became exceedingly fair" (3 Ne. 2:14–16). It is noteworthy that the children of these unions—in other words, the "young men and . . . daughters" of one light-skinned Nephite parent and one dark-skinned Lamanite parent—are described as becoming whiter, not darker.[12] The reason for this, according to the logic of the text, appears to be that the Lamanites adopted the more righteous ways of the Nephites, and this is mirrored in their children's lighter complexion. When the situation is reversed, and the Nephites pair off with wicked Lamanites, the intermingling results in children who inherit a "skin of blackness" (2 Ne. 5:21–23). Light-skin genes, again according to the logic of the text, appear to be dominant when the parents are righteous, and dark-skinned genes when the parents are wicked. It is not difficult to see how such passages could contribute to harmful attitudes toward persons of color in modern times.

Elsewhere, Mormon suggests that faithful Nephites become even whiter as a result of their interaction with Christ. Recording the events of the Savior's visit to the Nephites, Mormon writes:

> The light of his [Christ's] countenance did shine upon them, and behold they were as white as the countenance and also the garments of Jesus; and behold the whiteness thereof did exceed all the whiteness, yea, even there could be nothing upon earth so white as the whiteness thereof...and he did smile upon them again; and behold they were white, even as Jesus. (3 Ne. 19:25, 30)

While it is not immediately clear in this passage whether whiteness refers to luminosity or pigmentation, or whether the change was temporary or permanent, elsewhere in the Book of Mormon the correlation between light complexion and goodness is unambiguous. ☞ Apart from Jesus, the only other

☞ White as positive symbol appears in numerous places in the Book of Mormon. See 1 Nephi 8:11; 11:8, 13; 12:10–11; Alma 5:21, 24, 27; 13:11–12; 34:36; Ether 13:10.

(non-Nephite) persons described as light-skinned are Jesus's mother and the Gentiles who are led by God to the promised land. Mary, Nephi₁ tells us, "was exceedingly fair and white," and the Gentiles "were white, and exceedingly fair and beautiful, like unto my people before they were slain" (1 Ne. 11:13; 13:15). It is abundantly clear, therefore, that the Book of Mormon correlates light complexion and divine favor.

Mormon's discussion of skin color, however, resists reduction to mere racist ideology.[13] After all, the Nephites and Lamanites were equally descendants of Sariah and Lehi. Also, it is telling that when Mormon describes himself as a "pure descendant of Lehi" in an effort to authorize himself in the eyes of his readers, he clarifies that this means that he is a person who has kept the Lord's commandments and is an heir to his promises (3 Ne. 5:20–26). In other words, he understands the purity of his kinship to Lehi more in reference to his covenantal relationship with God than to his genealogy, race, or complexion.

The Book of Mormon also explicitly condemns bigotry in several places. Echoing Pauline language, Nephi₁, for instance, teaches that Christ "denieth none that come unto him, black and white, bond and free, male and female; and he remembereth the heathen; and all are alike unto God, both Jew and Gentile" (2 Ne. 26:33). And Jacob commands the Nephites to "revile no more against" the Lamanites "because of the darkness of their skins," explaining that they are "more righteous than you" (Jacob 3:5, 9). Jacob demonstrates here that skin color fails as a reliable reflection of divine favor almost as soon as it is established as one. Finally, as Richard Bushman has observed, "All the derogatory descriptions of the Lamanites notwithstanding," they still emerge in the Book of Mormon as "God's chosen people" and ultimate heirs of his promises.[14] Bushman's insight suggests that a proper reading of Nephite/Lamanite identity and social dynamics must take into account God's ultimate design for the Lamanites in the Book of Mormon: they come out on top. [15]

While it is not uncommon for ancient scriptural texts to correlate physical appearance and divine favor (e.g., Lev. 19:19, 27; 21:5; 1 Cor. 11:14–15; 1 Tim. 2:9; 1 Pet. 3:3), by modern standards, the assumption that a person's standing before God may be ascertained by their appearance is problematic. One reason this assumption is problematic is that persons have limited agency in how they look. We do not choose the color of our skin, for example, nor is it changed in accordance with our righteousness. Thus, to consider a person morally or ontologically inferior on such a basis undermines the role of human agency in the plan of salvation as well as the notion of a God who is no "respecter to persons" (Moro. 8:12; Acts 10:34). Another reason is that prescribed standards of appearance vary culturally and change over time. For instance, while Mormon depicts men with shaved heads as morally suspect (3 Ne. 4:7; Mosiah 10:8; Alma 3:5), Luke frames the apostle Paul's shaved head as a sign of his consecration to God (Acts 21:24). This example demonstrates that the significance of the same physical attribute can vary according to cultural context. What is indecorous, unnatural, extreme, or counter-cultural in one place and time may be completely innocuous, a sign of piety, or a tool for cultivating Christlikeness in another.

A final problem of assuming too close a relationship between physical appearance and God's approval is that some scriptures portray God as not caring very much about how his chosen people look. When the prophet Samuel was commanded to anoint a new king in Israel, his first inclination was to evaluate candidates based on their appearance: who outwardly appears most fit to be king. The Lord, however, corrected him, saying, "Look not on his countenance, or on the height of his stature...for the Lord seeth not as man seeth; for man looketh on the outward appearance, but the Lord looketh on the heart" (1 Sam. 16:7).

While the correlation between divine favor, physical appearance, and genealogy pervades the Book of Mormon, at the height of the Nephites' righteousness in 3–4 Nephi, chosenness is similarly determined by the character of the heart. As I will discuss in more detail in this book's final chapter, Mormon criticizes those with too narrow an understanding of "family" and "kindred" (3 Ne. 7:2, 4, 14) and praises those who align their conception of kinship with Christ's (4 Ne. 1:17). What Christ offers is a new kind of kinship, according to which being "heirs to the kingdom of God" is not a birthright; it is the result of adoption (4 Ne. 1:17). In this sense, the Lord's people are not chosen because of who they are; they are chosen because of what they have become in Christ. Disciples' identity as "children of God" transcends all earthly cultural identity, demonstrating, as the theologian Lactantius (ca. 250–325 AD) taught, that "the bond which unites our souls is stronger than the bond which unites our bodies."[16]

Having now explored Mormon's understanding of human nature as it relates to God and others, we are now in a position to examine human potential: what precisely it means to become like Christ.

3

Spiritual Development

Any accounting of spiritual development must address at least three things: ① human nature, ② human potential, and ③ the means by which to bridge the gap between the two. While the previous chapter examined human nature in some detail, this chapter focuses on 3–4 Nephi's conception of human moral potential and the cultivation of Christlikeness. A fundamental assumption of all moral discourse in the Book of Mormon is that God's creation of humankind did not end in Eden. Rather, God continually forms his disciples throughout the course of their lives. This is evident in the numerous statements in which Mormon speaks of spiritually maturing persons as becoming new creatures, as children of God, as being born again, as experiencing a mighty change of heart, and as receiving God's image in their countenance (e.g., Mosiah 27:25–6; Alma 5:14, 26, 49; 7:14). Such passages suggest that one hallmark of Christian discipleship is change: the persistent reorientation of the self toward God. The disciple, in other words, must master the art of becoming.

In the following pages, I examine some of the contours of this process of becoming: the role of commandments and divine aid, different moral virtues, the nature of perfection, and some signs of spiritual progress. The books of 3–4 Nephi are particularly fruitful for examining spiritual development because in them Christ arguably reveals more about both himself (i.e., the goal of development) and his doctrine (i.e., the means of

Universal Commandments in 3 Nephi

Commandment	Example scripture references
Keep the commandments	3 Ne. 12: 20; 14:21; 15:10; 18:33; 23:4
Repent	3 Ne. 9: 13; 11:32; 27:20; 30:2
Believe in Christ	3 Ne. 11: 32
Be converted	3 Ne. 9: 13
Offer a broken heart and contrite spirit	3 Ne. 9: 20
Come/return unto Christ	3 Ne. 9: 13; 10:6; 12:20; 21:6; 24:7; 27:20; 30:2
Do away with contention/ be reconciled with others	3 Ne. 11: 30; 12:24–25
Become as a little child	3 Ne. 11: 37–38
Be baptized	3 Ne. 11: 37–38; 21:6; 27:20; 30:2
Care for the needy	3 Ne. 12: 42; 13:1–3
Fast	3 Ne. 13: 16–17
Pray	3 Ne. 13: 5–9; 18:15, 18, 21, 23; 19:6, 17, 26; 20:31
Gather and worship	3 Ne. 18: 22
Search the scriptures	3 Ne. 10: 4; 20:11; 23:1; 23:5
Be a good example to others	3 Ne. 12: 13–16; 18:24
Keep thoughts and desires pure	3 Ne. 12: 29
Don't swear oaths	3 Ne. 12: 33–37
Don't retaliate	3 Ne. 12: 39
Be willing to offer more help to the needy than is requested	3 Ne. 12: 40–44
Love your enemies	3 Ne. 12: 44

FIGURE 2

Commandment	Example scripture references
Bless them that hurt you	3 Ne. 12: 44
Do good to them that hate you	3 Ne. 12: 44
Remember Christ's words	3 Ne. 13: 25
Seek first the kingdom of God and his righteousness	3 Ne. 13: 33
Judge not	3 Ne. 14: 1
Purify yourself	3 Ne. 14: 5; 20:41
Respect sacred things	3 Ne. 14: 6; 29:5, 7
Ask God for what you need	3 Ne. 14: 7; 17:3; 27:29
Do unto others what you would have them do unto you	3 Ne. 14: 12
Enter the strait gate	3 Ne. 14: 13; 27:33
Beware of false prophets	3 Ne. 14: 15
Look unto Christ	3 Ne. 15: 9
Endure to the end	3 Ne. 15: 9
Observe the sacrament worthily	3 Ne. 18: 1–12, 28, 30; 20:4
Deny none from worshipping unless they are unrepentant	3 Ne. 18: 22, 31
Preach Christ to others	3 Ne. 18: 25
Take upon yourself the name of Christ and worship in his name	3 Ne. 27: 5, 7, 9
Be like Jesus	3 Ne. 27: 21, 27
Be perfect	3 Ne. 12: 48

development) than he does anywhere else in the Book of Mormon. As will become clear in the following pages, in much the same way that Mormon portrays Christ and human nature in relational terms throughout 3–4 Nephi, spiritual development appears as collaboration between God and one another.

commandments

Cultivating Christlikeness requires understanding the purpose of commandments. Even a cursory glance at the Book of Mormon is enough to see the importance placed on obedience to divine imperatives: those who keep God's commandments are blessed; those who do not are punished. In 3 Nephi alone, Jesus issues approximately one hundred and fifty commands (averaging almost three per page). Some of these are universal mandates addressed to "all men, everywhere," such as "love your enemies," "repent," and "pray always" (3 Ne. 11:32; 12:44; 18:15, 18; 27:20). Others are "occasional," meaning applicable only to certain persons in a given moment in time, such as when Jesus forbids the Nephites from recording some of the things they witnessed while he was among them, or when he commands them to preserve the words of Samuel the Lamanite (3 Ne. 23:13; 26:16; 27:23; 28:14). In such passages, Mormon obviously does not expect the reader to go and do likewise. FIGURE 2 (previous pages) represents the commands in 3–4 Nephi that appear applicable in all times and places.

Commandments in 3–4 Nephi, as elsewhere in scripture, are theologically significant because they describe the things that one must do or not do in order to find favor in God's sight. They thus calibrate the reader to what is right and wrong. Just as importantly, however, they also serve as tools for transformation in that they are intended to pattern one's thoughts and behavior in a way that facilitates spiritual maturation. In this sense, obedience (i.e., actions) and virtue (i.e., the attributes of the actor) are inseparably connected in Mormon's thinking. A proper understanding of spiritual development as taught in 3–4 Nephi, therefore, must account for the fact that obedience to commandments is not an end in itself but a means to an end. For this reason, the ways in which obedience is made transformative is worthy of the disciple's attention. Christ stresses the importance of two specific dimensions of obedience for spiritual development: motivations and sincerity.

motivations

Motivations are crucial for unlocking the transformative power of obedience. For example, in his sermon to the Nephites, Jesus censures those who do alms "before men to be seen of them," who pray in order to "be seen of men," and who "disfigure their faces that they may appear unto men to fast" (3 Ne. 13:1, 5, 16). In these instances, the motivation for obedience—appearing righteous to others—is clearly not ideal, and Jesus condemns it as a goal unworthy of pursuit. Persons so motivated, he argues, "have their reward" in the form of the "glory of men" (3 Ne. 13:2, 5, 16). He further explains that improper motivations can also disqualify one from receiving God's intended blessings (3 Ne. 13:1–18). The underlying theological principle here is that God reserves his highest blessings for those who do the right things for the right reasons.

What then are proper motivations for obedience? Were one to establish a hierarchy of proper motivations based on 3–4 Nephi, it might look something like the following. At the bottom would be fear, either of God, humans, death, or punishment. For example, after listening to the prophecies of Lachoneus regarding their imminent destruction, the Nephites were struck with fear "insomuch that they did repent of all their sins"

(3 Ne. 3:16, 25). In this passage, fear of death and of the Gadianton robbers drives the Nephites to renew their commitment to God, which results in their deliverance from harm (3 Ne. 4). Elsewhere, Jesus interprets the words of Malachi and frames fear (of the Lord in this case) as a powerful and legitimate motivator for righteousness (3 Ne. 24:16). The implication is that fear can contribute to spiritual development, if one responds to it in the proper way. Mormon suggests elsewhere that this involves allowing it to have "full sway" in the heart, such that one is "[brought] down to the dust in humility" and reoriented to God (Alma 42:30). Mormon, however, never depicts fear as the ideal impetus for obedience.

A slightly more noble incentive on the hierarchy of motivations is the desire for a righteous reward. A consistent theme in 3–4 Nephi is that blessings follow righteousness (3 Ne. 5:22). Accordingly, a substantial portion of Jesus's sermon to the Nephites is framed in terms of cause and effect: if you do X, then Y will happen. For example: "blessed are all they who do hunger and thirst after righteousness, for they shall be filled with the Holy Ghost," "blessed are the merciful, for they shall obtain mercy," and "blessed are all the pure in heart, for they shall see God" (3 Ne. 12:6–8). By framing his teachings in this way, Jesus presents the reward for obedience as an acceptable incentive for righteousness. Consequently, when his nine Nephite disciples request to enter his kingdom at the end of their service, he responds: "Blessed are ye because ye desired this thing of me" (3 Ne. 28:3). He recognizes and honors his followers' desire to be blessed for their obedience.

At the same time, however, Jesus declares "more blessed" his other three disciples, who desired to remain on the earth in order to "bring the souls of men" unto him (3 Ne. 28:7, 9). In this case, the disciples' primary motivation for doing good is not receiving a reward for

49

their righteousness. It is love for God and others—this is the ideal. One is righteous not out of fear or in anticipation of compensation but because one possesses a Christlike love, and, thus, righteous acts and desires are organic expressions of one's character. Love becomes a kind of gravitational force, pushing the disciple to do and be good.[1] Love is of central importance in the Book of Mormon. It is what motivates the Father to provide a Savior for the world (1 Ne. 11; Alma 24:14). It is what motivates the Son to suffer and die for humankind (1 Ne 19:9; 2 Ne. 26:24; Ether 12:33–34). And, as Mormon's son would later teach, it "endureth forever," as do those who possess it (Moro. 7:47).

Significantly, however, Mormon suggests that the kind of love alluded to here does not necessarily originate with the disciple. Rather, it is frequently described as something that one is "filled" with (Mosiah 2:4; 4:12; Alma 38:12; Moro. 7:48). In other words, while one may possess Christlike love, its original source is external to the human soul; it is poured in from without. This kind of love cannot be mustered independent of divine aid. It must be gifted, kindled, stoked, and sustained by God. So conceived, loving is a collaborative rather than individual endeavor, possible only through sympathy with God's own heart. By loving as God loves, agency is elevated to the level of divine action. It is ennobled, empowered, and made transformative.

sincerity

In addition to proper motivations, 3–4 Nephi stress the importance of sincerity for spiritual development. Whereas motivations relate to the "why" of obedience, sincerity relates to the "how." Consider as one example Christ's teaching on prayer: "when ye pray, use not vain repetitions, as the heathen, for they think that they shall be heard for their much speaking" (3 Ne. 13:7). The logic underlying this counsel is that the quality of an act influences its efficacy. In this case, prayer is rendered ineffective when it is offered insincerely. Or, put another way, how one prays is more important than how *much* one prays (3 Ne. 13:7). Jesus emphasizes the necessity of sincerity elsewhere as well, teaching that one must repent and come unto him with "full purpose of heart," meaning, at least, with complete intentionality (3 Ne. 10:6; 12:24; 18:32). Here again the notion that obedience is an end in itself is undermined. Merely going through the motions is insufficient because it precludes the possibility of unlocking obedience's transformative potential. Christlikeness is the goal; sincere obedience is a means.

The relationship between sincerity and the efficacy of obedience has significant implications for spiritual development. Most importantly perhaps, this relationship demands that disciples learn the "science" of sincerity. As Jesus's sermon to the Nephites suggests, a challenge of habituating one's self to following the commandments is that obedience can become routine, robotic, or meaningless (3 Ne. 12:1–7; 16–18). This is not entirely problematic. The habit of daily service, for example, can accomplish much good in the world independent of the giver's intentions. One is thus reminded that God's commandments are typically intended to profit more than just those who obey them. When it comes to cultivating Christlikeness, however, the disposition of the actor is just as important as the action. The science of sincerity concerns bringing these two things into conformity with one another. What does it require, for example, to always feel gratitude when one expresses thanks in prayer, or yearning when one petitions God, or godly sorrow each time a person repents, or to render service without murmuring? Just as often as not, I would argue, it requires effort.

This exertion can reveal us to ourselves, making bare our true inclinations, desires, and predilections. To use a metaphor, obedience can sometimes feel like writing with one's nondominant hand—awkward and inauthentic. This is normal and productive of growth. In such dissonance, we realize that we are not naturally disposed to love an enemy, for example, or to bless those who harm us, or to pray for those who despitefully use us (3 Ne. 12:44). We are forced to recognize our inability to be sincere on our own. Even sincerity, although by nature firmly rooted in the soul, often requires external aid for its cultivation. God must help us be who we need to be, in order for us to do what he wants us to do. As Paul says, "it is God which worketh in you both to will and to do of his good pleasure" (Philip. 2:13). Perhaps God working in us involves him bringing us to a fuller understanding of the gravity of our sins so that we can feel the remorse necessary to properly repent and "be converted" (3 Ne. 9:13). Or maybe he will make his hand in our happiness more visible so that we can pray with "praise and thanksgiving" (3 Ne. 10:10). It may entail an endowment of discernment and love so that we can empathize with others and truly "mourn with those that mourn" (Mosiah 18:9).

God's role in human spiritual development undermines the notion that we can become like Christ by ourselves. In the same way that the Book of Mormon imagines ideal Christian personhood as relational, so spiritual development is framed as collaboration between the disciple, God, and other persons. Almost every commandment given by Jesus in 3–4 Nephi relates directly or indirectly to how humans view and interact with each other. In this sense, the Book of Mormon postures itself against what might be called *moral narcissism*,[2] by which I mean ① an overly robust estimation of one's ability to independently effect spiritual growth and ② undue attention to one's own spiritual development, at the neglect of others'. The disciple's growth in sanctity is predicated upon principles of interdependence, core-sponsibility, and other-centeredness. For this reason, spiritual development often occurs as a byproduct of selflessly seeking the welfare of others. As one English clergyman put it, Christlikeness is "received as a gift by those who are more interested in being disciples than in receiving rewards."[3]

Because humans are irrevocably implicated in one another's moral formation, relationships are like a laboratory in which we are molded to God's image. It is one thing to make plans for ourselves to help us to become better people: quiet scripture study, thoughtful prayer, regular fasting, and so on. It is quite another to allow the needs of others to dictate our daily spiritual exercise.[4] In practical terms, 3–4 Nephi provide a sense for what this kind of discipleship looks like: mutual forgiveness, social equality, care for the needy, love, fidelity, honesty, generosity, mercy, and suspension of judgement. Writing centuries later and on the other side of the world, the early Christian poet Narsai (ca. 399–502 AD) similarly stressed the importance of outward-facing discipleship when he wrote, "No one enters [God's kingdom] until he causes another to enter with him, for that is what this world demands of the one entering it. The doorkeeper will ask the one who approaches: 'Is there someone with you?' He will enter if there is someone and will remain outside if there is no one."[5]

character

The close relationship between doing and becoming in 3–4 Nephi reminds us that human beings are malleable. As the theologian Gregory of Nyssa (335–394 AD) taught, "Human nature came into being as something capable of becoming whatever it determines upon, and to whatever goal the thrust of its choice leads, it undergoes alteration

Parts	Negative Qualities	Positive Qualities
Heart	Hard, wicked, proud, stout, stubborn, fat, false, unsteady, corrupt, uncircumcised, turned from God	Soft, pure, sanctified, poor, broken, lowly, open, one, great, full, holy, turned to God
Mind	Carnal, blind, sore, frenzied, deranged	Spiritual, sober, pure, firm, delicate, diligent
Soul	Drooped in sin, wounded, damned, corrupt, hungry, thirsty	Awake, redeemed, spotless, at rest, illuminated, expanded, enlarged, swelled, filled, saved, at peace, sure, steadfast
Spirit	Contentious, wicked, lying, evil, bad	Contrite, firm, strong, unconquerable, noble, poor, good, free
Flesh	Full of darkness	Sanctified, holy, full of light

FIGURE 3 Human parts and their negative and positive qualities

in accord with what it seeks."[6] When we seek Christ, we become like him. But what precisely does this look like? What specific attributes are we to cultivate? To what degree is reaching our moral potential possible in mortality? And what are some of the signs that we are on the right path?

human moral potential
Mormon speaks of human moral potential in different ways. For example, at times he maps moral attributes onto the individual parts of the inner person, as illustrated (see FIGURE 3).

As may be seen in FIGURE 3, Mormon provides a key for exploring what it means to be a good or bad person on the most fundamental level. It is incumbent upon us as disciples to actualize our positive moral potential because character informs conduct. As Jesus explains to the Nephites, "Every good tree bringeth forth good fruit; but a corrupt tree bringeth forth evil fruit. A good tree cannot bring forth evil fruit, neither a corrupt tree bring forth good fruit" (3 Ne. 14:17–18).

In 3–4 Nephi, Mormon also periodically discusses moral attributes independent of their relation to the parts of the human self. He specifically references the qualities listed below:

Negative Qualities
Wickedness, vanity, blindness, unbelief, foolishness, hate, pride, anger, lust, deceit, mischievousness, cunning, hypocrisy, uncleanliness, contentiousness, not fearing of God, lasciviousness

Positive Qualities
Steadfastness, firmness, justice, God-fearing, righteousness, desiring righteousness, faithfulness, goodness, humility, diligence, immovableness, meekness, peacefulness, agreeableness, forgiving, fairness, love, compassion, cleanliness, mercy, wisdom, kindness, holiness, perfection

Frequently, such positive attributes are embodied in moral exemplars like Lachoneus, Gidgiddoni, or other unnamed Nephites and Lamanites (e.g., 3 Ne. 3–4, 6; 4 Ne. 1:29). At other times, Mormon speaks of moral character in more figurative or abstract language. For example, good persons are compared to or encouraged to be like children, light, salt, sheep, a wise man who built his house upon a rock, and a tree that bears good fruit (3 Ne. 9:22; 11:37–38; 12:13–14; 14:17–20, 24; 15:12, 24). In each case, the disciple is left to ponder how each symbol provides an aspirational vision of what humanity may achieve in Christ.

In Christian thought, it is not uncommon for theologians to reflect on the nature of different moral attributes and their relationship to another, posing such questions as, Which virtue is the greatest? Is there a hierarchy among the other virtues? And does the possession of one entail the possession of any other? While Mormon never reflects on the nature of virtue in such a systematic manner, one moral attribute stands out as unique in 3–4 Nephi: perfection. One of two instances in the Book of Mormon in which mortal human beings are commanded to be perfect appears in 3 Ne. 12:48 (see also Moro. 10:32–33). Before examining the nature of this attribute within the context of 3 Nephi, however, it will be helpful to first demonstrate how perfection is understood elsewhere in the Book of Mormon. This will provide a foundation for interpreting Jesus's injunction to "be perfect" (3 Ne. 12:48).

perfection

In the Book of Mormon, the word *perfect* is used primarily to describe three things. First, it refers to the degree to which certain moral attributes may be possessed. Nephi$_1$ and Mormon specifically mention "perfect" knowledge, faith, understanding, uprightness, love, honesty, and hope (2 Ne. 9:13–14, 23; 31:20; Jacob 4:12; 7:4; Alma 27:27; 48:11; 50:37; Moro. 8:26). To possess these attributes perfectly means to possess them completely. Second, the word may describe the physical human form following the resurrection. Mormon writes, "The spirit and the body shall be reunited again in its perfect form...restored to its perfect frame" (Alma 11:43–44). Here, perfection again denotes wholeness or completeness. That even wicked persons will be resurrected to their "perfect" form suggests that this perfection is physical, not moral (2 Ne. 9:16; Morm. 9:14). Finally, the word may be applied holistically to individual persons, with respect to both their moral and their physical state. The only persons described in the Book of Mormon as perfect in this sense are Christ and God (3 Ne. 12:48). ☛

Because Mormon believes that all persons will obtain physical perfection in the resurrection (Alma 40:16–19), the command to be perfect in 3 Nephi must refer primarily to one's moral state. After all, why would Jesus command a person to do something that would already occur by default? Moral perfection entails at least possessing all moral attributes in their fullness. This is distinct from sinlessness because it involves cultivating goodness, not just the absence of badness. Or, put another way, moral perfection includes but is not limited to the absence of sin. For this reason, young children are described as sinless and innocent in the Book of Mormon, but never as "perfect" (Mosiah 3:16–21; Moro. 8:5–22). The same may be said of Adam and Eve in Eden: they were sinless and innocent but still needed the experience of mortality to mature spiritually toward perfection (2 Ne. 2:19–24).

While Mormon portrays some persons as possessing individual virtues perfectly, no person in the Book of Mormon is shown to possess all of them simultaneously. This lack of perfect persons, in conjunction with Mormon's understanding of fallen human nature, suggests that attaining moral perfection in mortality is improbable, if not impossible, for disciples of Christ. And, theologically speaking, if such perfection were

☛ One significant difference between Christ's New Testament Sermon on the Mount and his sermon to the Nephites regards perfection. Whereas prior to his resurrection, Jesus commands the people to be perfect "even as your Father which is in heaven" (Matt. 5:48), following his resurrection, he adds "even as I, or your Father who is in heaven is perfect" (3 Ne. 12:48).

possible for us, Christ would be much less unique. In this sense, Mormon agrees with the Prophet Joseph Smith, who taught that "it will be a great while after you have passed through the veil" before one can learn all the principles of perfection.[7] Mormon's teachings thus suggest that the degree of perfection we can hope to attain in mortality entails primarily the victory over our temptations rather than their absence.

The fact that we cannot achieve moral perfection in this life then raises the question of why Christ would issue a commandment that cannot be obeyed in the present. What lessons might be learned in striving toward a currently unattainable ideal? Perhaps it is the case that our failed efforts to be perfect make us more aware of our dependence on God and on one another, thereby motivating us to participate in healthy support systems, appropriate accountability structures, empowering covenantal relationships, and to respond to our own and others' failings with patience and forgiveness.

Perhaps it is that striving for perfection helps us to see the inherent value of the pursuit. It teaches us that discipleship in life is about progress, not perfection. As the English poet Robert Browning wrote, "The aim, if reached or not, makes great the life."[8] The challenge we face as disciples, therefore, is discerning *proximate* ends—what we can currently achieve in our fallen state—from *ultimate ends*, or the final goal. It is also learning to resist the tendency to believe that we are defined by our failures, that we must be flawless to be worthy, that we can never do enough, or that our efforts are futile.[9] If failing to be perfect is the norm, then one of the disciple's most useful skills is the ability to learn from failure.

Pursuing perfection also provides a clearer sense of what perfection actually entails. While I have characterized moral perfection as the possession of all moral attributes in their fullness, one should not assume that defining the word is the same as understanding the attribute. Mormon teaches in several places that human language is inadequate in conveying certain spiritual truths. Regarding Jesus's prayer, for instance, we are told that the Nephites claimed that "no tongue can speak, neither can there be written by any man, neither can the hearts of men conceive so great and marvelous things as we both saw and heard Jesus speak" (3 Ne. 17:17). Elsewhere, Mormon records that the Nephite disciples lacked the "power" to "utter the things which they saw and heard" (3 Ne. 28:14). The Nephites' experiences demonstrate that some knowledge cannot be fully grasped by just the mind. Or, as one modern theologian put it, "It is rational to accept the limits of human rationality."[10]

The experience of childbirth may provide an apt analogy to further illustrate what I believe to be Mormon's point. A father who witnesses the birth of his children has some understanding of what giving birth entails. This knowledge, however, pales in comparison to the knowledge of the mother, for whom giving birth is an embodied experience. Some truths can be fully grasped only experientially. The same may be said of perfection. Because we are not yet perfect, our ability to understand what it entails is limited. The further we walk down the path of moral progress, however, the more clearly we can discern the destination. Perhaps this evolving understanding is what John and Moroni meant when they wrote that knowing the perfected Christ "as he is" involves us becoming "like him," "purified even as he is pure" (1 Jn. 3:2; Moro. 7:48).

The danger of assuming that we fully understand perfection is that this assumption can lead to an unwillingness to correct course—to seek out and accommodate new information, insight, and revelation. The imperfect disciple, therefore, must recognize that while what has been learned of perfection may be correct, it is also partial. One's current understanding should not, to quote Gregory of Nyssa again, "set limits to the object of the search" but should be "the starting point of a search after more exalted things."[11]

signs of progress

It would be impossible in such a brief volume to discuss the nature of each moral attribute mentioned in 3–4 Nephi. The remainder of this chapter, therefore, focuses instead on a few examples of how moral character is manifested more generally in a person's psychological operations. Having already addressed in the previous section how morality is mapped onto the five *parts* of the human being (heart, spirit, mind, soul, and body/flesh), this section explores how morality is manifested in the human *faculties* of cognition, emotion, and volition. It answers the following questions: According to 3–4 Nephi, what do good people think, feel, and desire? And how might such portrayals contribute to a fuller understanding of Christian discipleship and spiritual development?

cognition

Common cognitive expressions of spiritual maturity in 3–4 Nephi relate to a person's belief, knowledge, and memory. For example, righteous persons are portrayed as believing in Jesus, his teachings, his coming and the signs associated with it, and that he is God's son; they are also portrayed as believing in Jesus's disciples' preaching, in the Father and the Holy Ghost, and that God answers prayers (3 Ne. 1:7–22; 7:21; 9:17; 11:32–35; 12:1, 2 ,19; 16:6–7; 18:20; 19:20–23, 28; 20:31; 26:9–10; 28:18; 4 Ne. 1:29, 36–38). Such beliefs are never framed as ends in themselves but are expected to precipitate righteous conduct and moral renovation. Here again it becomes apparent that discipleship as Mormon imagines it is not a system of belief; it is a way of life, an art of existence. Additionally, it is rare for persons to believe such things without also facing some form of opposition or reasons not to believe. The Nephites who looked forward to the signs of Christ's birth, for example, "began to be very sorrowful," fearing that their faith might be in vain, when the signs did not appear as they anticipated (3 Ne. 1:7). The same people were subsequently threatened with death for their beliefs and yet maintained them (3 Ne. 1:11). Mormon, therefore, not only idealizes belief in things that are true but also praises belief that persists in uncertainty, doubt, and opposition.

There is not a significant difference in 3–4 Nephi between what spiritually maturing persons "believe" and what they "know." Parallels also exist in the factors that affect these cognitive functions. Sin and righteousness, for example, influence one's capacity to believe and know in negative and positive ways, respectively (3 Ne. 15:19–20). The Holy Spirit likewise plays a role, both facilitating and ratifying what is believed and known (3 Ne. 11:35; 12:2; 16:4; 21:2). Mormon suggests, however, that, unlike belief, knowledge comes in degrees. He thus distinguishes between knowing, on the one hand, and knowing "of a surety," on the other (3 Ne. 11:15). This distinction is noteworthy because it suggests that it is possible to know without "a surety," which challenges assumptions regarding the mutual exclusivity of doubt/uncertainty and knowledge. Knowledge "of a surety" is relatively uncommon in the Book of Mormon (see 1 Ne. 5:8; 17:55; Mosiah 7:14; Alma 5:45–46). And in 3–4 Nephi, the Nephites gain sure knowledge of Christ only when they "thrust their hands into his side, and . . . feel the prints of the nails in his hands and in his feet," seeing him "with their eyes" and touching him "with their hands" (3 Ne. 11:15). Christ, nevertheless, privileges belief over this surer form of knowledge, declaring "more blessed" those who believe and yet have never "seen me" nor "know that I am" (3 Ne. 12: 2; cf. John 20:29). In these verses, Christ demonstrates again the degree to which God values fidelity in uncertainty. Uncertainty, Mormon argues, is a tool used by God to bless his children and to test their faith, so that "greater things" might be revealed to them (3 Ne. 26:9–11). Uncertainty is both natural and spiritually productive.

Mormon also frames the act of remembering as an expression of spiritual maturity. Good persons remember Christ, his body, and his teachings (3 Ne. 15:1; 18:7, 11; 20:11; 27:12). This type of remembering seems to entail more than just conducting a cognitive inventory. As Brett Thomas has observed, in the Book of Mormon remembrance is often depicted as a means to motivate, to spark hope, to break the heart and make contrite the spirit, to build faith, or to instill fear.[12] Remembering, therefore, is not only a manifestation of spiritual maturity but also a spiritual exercise, a way to enlist the past in the present struggle for transformation. Mormon's emphasis on transformative remembering gestures toward the notion that goodness is transitory and that it must be consistently pursued to be possessed. For this reason, disciples are to "always" reach out to Christ in their minds, to recall who he is, what he has done, and what he can do (3 Ne. 18:7, 11). They are to extend themselves back and to dwell, if even for a small moment, in experiences that have passed but that remain useful for orienting the soul to God.

emotion

One's moral state may also be reflected in one's emotions. Sorrow for the sins of others is the most common emotional expression of spiritual maturity in

3–4 Nephi. Mormon records numerous examples of sorrow for others' sins. In 3 Ne. 1 he writes that "when Nephi, the son of Nephi, saw this wickedness of his people, his heart was exceedingly sorrowful" (3 Ne. 1:10). Elsewhere, Nephi₃ is "grieved for the hardness of their hearts and the blindness of their minds" (3 Ne. 7:16). Jesus is also said to have "groaned within himself" for the wickedness of Israel and laments that they are led away captive by the devil (3 Ne. 17:14; 27:32). While Mormon refers to the disciples' path to God as the "great plan of happiness," it is evident from these passages that Christlikeness is not equivalent to happiness as we typically understand it (Alma 42:8, 16; see also Hel. 13:38). Rather, Mormon suggests that sorrow is one byproduct of a Christlike love. A Christlike person cannot help but love, and cannot both love what is imperfect and avoid sorrow. For this reason, the three Nephite disciples who were changed "that they might not taste of death" were able to avoid all pain and sorrow that mortal humans experience, "save it [were] for the sins of the world" (3 Ne. 28:9, 38).

Correspondingly, Mormon also portrays joy in others' spiritual welfare as a sign of moral maturity. For instance, observing the faith of the righteous Nephites, Jesus weeps and says, "now behold, my joy is full" (3 Ne. 17:20). And prior to his departure from the people, he tells them: "And now, behold, my joy is great, even unto fulness, because of you, and also this generation; yea, and even the Father rejoiceth, and also all the holy angels, because of you" (3 Ne. 27:30). It is telling that Jesus's fullest joy emerges from the successes of others. Here again, Mormon alludes to the relationship between other-centeredness and discipleship. If the disciple's fullest joy is to be predicated upon others' spiritual welfare, then attentiveness to the spiritual welfare of others must be central to achieving the goal of God's plan of "happiness." Furthermore, the emotional sympathy between the disciple and others suggests that spiritual growth is a movement toward oneness with others. As one German philosopher insightfully wrote, "when once compassion is stirred within me by another's pain, then his weal and woe go straight to my heart, exactly in the same way, if not always to the same degree, as otherwise I feel only my own. Consequently, the difference between myself and him is no longer an absolute one."[13]

Mormon's idealization of certain emotional responses is sobering, especially because people cannot always choose how they feel in any given moment. Emotions, in other words, are not typically matters of the will and, therefore, cannot be easily manufactured in accordance with what is morally praiseworthy. It is not likely Mormon's goal, then, to get his readers to mimic what is praiseworthy but inauthentic. Rather, he invites us to consider the way in which our emotions may reveal us to ourselves. Emotional responses can be barometers of character precisely because they are so authentic. The disciple might therefore ask, How do I feel when someone fails where I have succeeded? How do I feel when someone succeeds where I have failed? Am I the kind of person who feels praiseworthy emotions?

volition

As previously mentioned, the most noble volitional expression represented in 3–4 Nephi is the desire to bring souls to Christ (3 Ne. 28:7–9, 29). Other laudable desires include the desire to dwell with God, to come unto Christ, to know his works, to be baptized, and to receive the Holy Ghost (3 Ne. 11:23; 12:23; 17:8; 19:9; 28:2). These may be contrasted with the desires of the wicked, who seek after power, authority, riches, and the vain things of the world (3 Ne. 6:15). Mormon believes that, not unlike knowledge, desire comes in degrees. He thus specifies that persons must come unto Christ with "full purpose of heart," which implies something beyond the superficial or perfunctory (3 Ne. 10:6; 12:24; 18:32). He also demonstrates that the cultivation of righteous desires is not the responsibility of the lone individual. Rather, God may implant desires in a person, such as in the case of the Nephites, who upon receiving the Holy Ghost, "were filled with desire" (3 Ne. 19:24). This is encouraging, given that sometimes the most the disciple can do is want to want.

Desire is theologically significant in the Book of Mormon because it enables choice. As Nephi$_1$ writes, one must first be "enticed" (a form of desire) before choice can exist (2 Ne. 2:15–16; see also Moro. 7:12–13). Choice, in turn, leads to action, and action facilitates transformation. Righteous desire is thus the fountain of all moral conduct and spiritual development. For this reason, Mormon frames volitional union with God as a sign of advanced spiritual maturity. By volitional union, I do not mean merely doing what God says; I mean wanting what God wants. Such seemed to be the case with Nephi, who was told by God that "all things shall be done unto thee according to thy word, for thou shalt not ask that which is contrary to my will" (Hel. 10:5).

The argument may be made, however, that baser desires play just as significant a role as noble ones do in the disciple's spiritual journey. It is not uncommon for conflicting desires, or what one philosopher refers to as "lower-order" and "higher-order" desires,[14] to coexist within a person.[15] When someone fasts, for example, the desire both to eat and to not eat are simultaneously present, and part of the spiritual power of fasting comes from prioritizing the latter desire over the former. The same may be said of any temptation or sin that is denied for the sake of something good. In the same way that physical muscles grow in response to resistance, so spiritual muscles may be built by doing good things we don't want to do, and by not doing bad things we do want to do (see Rom. 7:14–25). The underlying principle is that growth and righteousness frequently emerge from struggle.

Jesus's atoning sacrifice aptly illustrates the interplay of competing desires in the disciple's journey toward God. Mormon teaches that Jesus lived a fully human life, experiencing "pains and afflictions and temptations of every kind" (Alma 7:11). In accordance with his experience of the human condition, Christ acknowledges several times that, in Gethsemane, some part of him did not desire to suffer. After all, what human desires to suffer? In Matthew, for instance, he prays, "O my Father, if it be possible, let this cup pass from me," and in the Doctrine and Covenants he frankly states, "[I] would that I might not drink the bitter cup" (Matt. 26:39; D&C 19:18). We might call Jesus's desire to avoid suffering and death a lower-order desire. Also present within him, however, was the competing desire to do God's will, hence his prayer's conclusion: "nevertheless not as I will, but as thou wilt" (Matt. 26:39). By aligning his higher-order, or behavior-determining, desires, with God's will, he demonstrated an important truth of discipleship. Obeying God with full purpose of heart need not always entail an energetic leap into righteousness. Sometimes it is a quiet, almost reluctant, surrender to the heat of the "refiner's fire" and sting of the "fuller's soap" (3 Ne. 24:2).

4

Society

It may be helpful at this point to remind the reader of where we have been. Over the past three chapters, I have examined 3–4 Nephi's portrayal of Christ, human nature, and the cultivation of Christlikeness. Along the way, I have attempted to demonstrate the ways in which Christlikeness finds its fullest expression in community, collaboration, and collectivity. From the most basic facets of human identity and through all stages of spiritual development, Christ's relational nature is reflected in the disciple. This chapter will turn more directly to the implications of Christian discipleship for public life and will ask the question, How might one work toward a more ideal society based on the teachings of 3–4 Nephi?

Mormon records that Christ's coming to the Nephites inaugurated a centuries-long period of peace, prosperity, and righteousness in Nephite society. During these years, the Nephites and those who lived among them sought to govern themselves according to principles that allowed them to flourish temporally and spiritually. Thus, 3–4 Nephi provides a glimpse of the "ideal" society as Mormon imagines it. In addition to providing a historical account of the development of Nephite society, Mormon takes seriously the notion that Christian discipleship should inform one's conduct in the public sphere. For this reason, his record is both descriptive and didactic. He expects that the reader will come to his record with the question, What should I do to be like God's people? He responds by enumerating three characteristics of the ideal society: all things in common, equal access to great learning, and unity. By presenting Nephite society as both a light on a hill and a work in progress, Mormon provides the reader with a path toward the ideal.

all things in common

The first characteristic of the ideal society according to Mormon is that all persons would voluntarily have "all things in common," meaning that material resources—in other words, "goods" and "substance"—would be distributed in such a way that there would be no rich or poor in society (3 Ne. 26:19; 4 Ne. 1:3, 25). Mormon does not appear to advocate a one-time divestiture of property, as described in Luke 18:22, but instead advises periodic and sustainable acts of giving as circumstances in the community dictate. And rather than writing that all persons possessed the same amount of resources, he suggests that everyone had sufficient resources for their needs and dealt justly one with another (3 Ne. 26:19). In this sense, the Nephites appear to have practiced something akin to the early Christian practice described in Acts 2:44.[1]

The accumulation of wealth is not presented as inherently wrong in 3–4 Nephi, nor do these books idealize the total renunciation of wealth. Rather, wealth is one way in which God blesses the faithful, and economic prosperity is frequently, although not always, correlated to righteousness. For example, Mormon writes in 4 Nephi that the Nephites "had become exceedingly rich, because of their prosperity in Christ" (4 Ne. 1:23). In this passage, riches are the direct consequence of fidelity to God. Elsewhere, however, Mormon acknowledges that poverty, not unlike fasting and prayer, can dispose one to virtues like humility and lowliness of heart (3 Ne. 6:12–13; see also

Alma 32:2–4, 12–15). For this reason, the poor are frequently portrayed as righteous in the Book of Mormon. This is merely to say that financial status is not a reliable metric of divine favor in the Book of Mormon. Wealth becomes an obstacle to discipleship when it is pursued for its own sake, or when it leads to pride, vanity, social inequality, priestcraft, maltreatment of the less advantaged, or other sins. This occurs more often than not (e.g., 3 Ne. 6:10; 4 Ne. 1:24–25, 41, 46).

Having all things in common requires a proper understanding of the nature of wealth and of the attitude the disciple should have toward it. God intends wealth to always move toward those in need, and Jesus would have the Nephites align their desires with its force of motion. He teaches them that the proper use of wealth assumes a particular disposition of soul. Perhaps for this reason, he instructs the Nephites to prioritize "the kingdom of God and his righteousness" over the pursuit of the earth's material resources (3 Ne. 13:33). For in so doing, one learns how to righteously navigate affluence. People are to be stewards, not owners, of the earth's resources (3 Ne. 9:15; 24:8–12; see also Mosiah 4:22), and they have an obligation to both care for others and be willing to give more than is requested of them—for example, to provide also a "cloak" when only a "coat" is petitioned (3 Ne. 12:40, 42).[2] As the Christian theologian Jerome (ca. 347–420 AD) observed, "It manifests greater love to offer what you are not bound to give than to surrender what is required of you."[3] The words of one of Jerome's contemporaries, Evagrius of Pontus (ca. 345–399 AD), are also apt here: "It is good to show beneficence to all, but more so to those unable to return the favor."[4]

Additionally, true disciples are not to pursue or embrace the honor that can accompany the "fine things of the world" or their philanthropic distribution (4 Ne.

1:24). Rather, caring for the needy should be done in a way that does not draw attention to the giver; as Jesus says, "Do not your alms before men to be seen of them" (3 Ne. 13:1). Echoing again his Sermon on the Mount in the Gospel of Matthew, he adds, "When thou doest alms let not thy left hand know what thy right hand doeth," suggesting that the giver should also avoid being too reflective about the goodness of their own charitable conduct (3 Ne. 13:3). Ideally, ministering to the disadvantaged should be motivated by compassion and love, and not by a desire to enhance one's status.

One great challenge that God's people face in 3–4 Nephi is how to remain faithful when things are going well. It is perhaps easy enough to sincerely turn to God when all seems hopeless, in famine of body and spirit. In times of abundance, however, it can be difficult to muster the zeal to love God with all the heart, might, mind, and strength. Spiritual fervor, Mormon suggests, often burns hottest in affliction. As Brigham Young taught of the Saints in his day, "This people will stand mobbing, robbing, poverty, and all manner of persecution, and be true. But my greater fear for them is that they cannot stand wealth."[5]

While it is not made explicit in 3–4 Nephi, Mormon expresses this very concern elsewhere in the large plates. He laments:

> We may see at the very time when he [God] doth prosper his people, yea, in the increase of their fields, their flocks and their herds, and in gold, and in silver, and in all manner of precious things of every kind and art...yea, and in fine, doing all things for the welfare and happiness of his people; yea, then is the time that they do harden their hearts, and do forget the Lord their God, and do trample under their feet the Holy

One—yea, and this because of their ease, and
their exceedingly great prosperity. (Hel. 12:2)

Mormon's discussion of the relationship between faithfulness and wealth in 3–4 Nephi is clearly informed by
this way of thinking. Accordingly, he presents humility, justice, and generosity as indispensable qualities of
those blessed with abundance. One reason for this is
that these attributes resist the tendency toward self-re-
gard and the valuation of things over people. He also
implies elsewhere that retaining in remembrance the
source of one's blessings (i.e., God) and the reason for
which they are given (i.e., righteousness) is necessary
to remain faithful in times of abundance (Hel. 12:1–26).
Without these virtues and practices, Mormon teaches,
"riches, and the vain things of the world" can seduce and
enslave the soul (3 Ne. 6:15).

   The appropriate use of wealth not only requires certain moral qualities but also promotes their cultivation.
Mormon alludes specifically to the attributes of freedom, equality, justice, unity, peace, humility, and righteousness, which he correlates to the faithful Nephites'
economic practices (3 Ne. 26:19; 4 Ne. 1:3–4, 17). In 4
Nephi he describes some of the blessings of the proper
use of wealth in the following way:

   And they had all things common among them;
   therefore there were not rich and poor, bond
   and free, but they were all made free, and par-
   takers of the heavenly gift....And it came to
   pass that there was no contention in the land,
   because of the love of God which did dwell in
   the hearts of the people. And there were no
   envyings, nor strifes, nor tumults, nor whore-
   doms, nor lyings, nor murders, nor any manner of lasciviousness; and surely there could

not be a happier people among all the people who had been created by the hand of God.
(4 Ne. 1:3, 15–16)

This passage demonstrates that 3–4 Nephi's discussion of social welfare is about more than economics and equality. It also is about forming the soul and society in God's image. Having all things in common extends from and leads to peace and harmony with God and one another.

In traditional Christian thought the rich and poor have something of a complimentary relationship, and one sees a comparable dynamic operative in 3–4 Nephi. The theologian John Chrysostom (ca. 349–407 AD), for instance, taught that the rich and the poor need each other: the poor depend on the rich for their temporal welfare, and the rich need the poor to fulfill God's command to care for the needy. This relationship, however, is not merely an exchange of treasure on earth for treasure in heaven. Rather, Chrysostom argues that this attentiveness to each other's needs "makes our love for one another more fervent."[6] In other words, growing in love is the goal. Mormon takes a similar approach in that he depicts the earth's resources as divinely designed tools for transformation and argues that Christlikeness is both a means to and an end of good stewardship over them.

Finally, it is significant that in 3–4 Nephi Mormon does not explicitly address common questions that may arise when caring for the poor. 🖛 For example, What precisely constitutes poverty? What if I am too poor to give? How can I know if the poor really deserve charity? What if the poor are trying to take advantage of me? How can I be sure that the poor will not squander what is given to them? What if I am enabling the

🖛 Mormon does address this question in Mosiah 4:24.

poor's dependence on others rather than helping them to become self-sufficient? Surely, Mormon's intent in 3–4 Nephi was not to provide a systematic treatise on charitable giving. However, I believe that what he does and does not say are equally telling. That he emphasizes the directive of love-motivated giving over possible exceptions to the rule suggests that if one is to err in caring for the needy, one would do well to err on the side of mercy.

equal access to great learning

The second characteristic of the ideal society as described in 3–4 Nephi is that all persons would have equal access to education, or as Mormon says, to "great learning" (3 Ne. 6:12). Here it becomes clear that Mormon is concerned not only with caring for the disadvantaged but also with eliminating the social structures that exploit and perpetuate poverty and inequality. Before addressing the importance of education in 3–4 Nephi it may be helpful to briefly define what Mormon likely means by "great learning." When learning, teaching, and knowledge are mentioned in the Book of Mormon, there seems to be a distinction between what might be termed "religious" education and a more "vocational" education. By *religious education*, I refer to familiarity with God's laws, religious texts, and the teachings of inspired persons (3 Ne. 6:18; 15:1; 22:13; 26:8, 19). By *vocational education* I mean training that enables one to perform a particular occupation in society, such as merchant, lawyer, officer, governor, or judge (3 Ne. 6:11, 19, 22).

The "great learning" to which Mormon refers in 3–4 Nephi appears to be of the latter sort. Thus, when he laments that the poor were "ignorant because of their poverty, and others did receive great learning because of their riches," it is not because the poor lacked knowledge of God; in fact, they are lauded for their humility, meekness, and penitence before God (3 Ne. 6:12–14). Rather, because of their economic disadvantage, they were denied "chances for learning" that would have enabled them to be more self-sufficient and to contribute to society in a greater variety of ways, including as leaders and policy makers (3 Ne. 6:12). And this appears to be one of the major points of Mormon's argument: unequal access to education undermines God's vision of a society in which all may contribute to the greater good and in which those in power prioritize God's will and the welfare of others.

Mormon tells us that the wealthier and more educated Nephites were failing as leaders because they lacked virtue and that the more virtuous Nephites could not lead because they lacked education. He records that great learning led many Nephites to be puffed up with pride, to ignore the counsels of God, and to exploit and persecute the less-advantaged to promote their own agenda (3 Ne. 6:10–30). It is not that these learned persons lacked religious education and just didn't know any better; "they knew the will of God concerning them, for it had been taught unto them; therefore they did wilfully rebel against God" (3 Ne. 6:18). Their problem, then, was not lack of truth; it was the failure to engage with truth in a transformative way. Consequently, through wickedness, favoritism, and nepotism, these individuals intentionally "set at defiance the law and the rights of their country; and they did covenant one with another to destroy the governor, and to establish a king over the land, that the land should no more be at liberty" (3 Ne. 6:27–30).

To be clear, Mormon does not say that equal access to education would have necessarily prevented the corruption of the powerful or the fracturing of society. However, as previously intimated, he implies that those who lacked educational opportunities typically excelled in the virtues that would have made great learning a benefit to cohesive society rather than a liability (3 Ne. 6:13). In other words, it was the "ignorant" who possessed faith, humility, and soft-heartedness, and who were obedient to God's commands (3 Ne. 6:12–13; see also 2 Ne. 9:28–29, 42). They were slow to anger and to retaliate, were "penitent before God," and would thus be more inclined to maintain "great order in the land" and to form "laws according to equity and justice" (3 Ne. 6:4, 13). And yet because of their poverty and lack of education, and thus their lack of social influence, their voices were silenced or fell on deaf ears. Knowledge gained through education, it would seem, is intended to be shared, to be made intelligible and constructive, and to be consecrated to the betterment of others.

At stake in 3–4 Nephi, then, is not just equal access to great learning but a social structure that enables all members of society to flourish without oppression and prevents preferential treatment of the rich. Mormon makes clear that wealth enables educational attainment, educational attainment impacts social class, social class affects influence, and influence promotes change, for better or for worse. What the Nephites also appear to have needed was more diversity of thought among thoughtful persons: a greater number of educated, influential, and faithful individuals who could speak loudly and to great effect in response to those who sought to undermine the "regulations of the government" and the ideals of the church (3 Ne. 7:6; 4 Ne. 1:40). Although Mormon lauds the merits of unity, he is painfully aware that the fracturing and fall of Nephite society occurred because of a great deal of like-mindedness, just not the good kind (3 Ne. 1:29; 6:27–30). The wicked Nephites, who, Mormon tells us, became "exceedingly more numerous than were the people of

God," were like a choir singing the wrong note in unison (4 Ne. 1:40).

The social psychologist Jonathan Haidt has recently argued that diversity, especially among policy makers and those in positions of authority, greatly contributes to a flourishing society because it functions to curtail harmful and unchecked like-mindedness. He writes:

> We should not expect individuals to produce good, open-minded, truth-seeking reasoning, particularly when self-interest or reputational concerns are in play. But if you put individuals together in the right way, such that some individuals can use their reasoning powers to disconfirm the claims of others, and all individuals feel some common bond or shared fact that allows them to interact civilly, you can create a group that ends up producing good reasoning as an emergent property of the social system. This is why it is important to have intellectual and ideological diversity within any group or institution whose goal is to find truth (such as an intelligence agency or a community of scientists) or to produce good public policy (such as a legislature or advisory board).[7]

The story of Nephite society may aptly serve as a cautionary tale of what can happen when individuals are not put together, as Haidt would say, "in the right way" or when those in power are more concerned with self-interest and reputation than with empowering, educating, and giving voice to the marginalized and disadvantaged.

unity

A third characteristic of the ideal society is unity, which can take various forms. Mormon's discussion of unity in

3–4 Nephi is complex, and at this point it is probably clear that not all unity is good and not all diversity is bad. As previously mentioned, sometimes Mormon negatively portrays unity, such as when many Nephites were united in their wickedness and subversion of the government (3 Ne. 6:29). At other times, he depicts diversity as beneficial to society. For instance, in 3 Nephi those identified as culturally distinct from the Nephites—in other words, the Lamanites—helped preserve the moral integrity of the Nephite church. Contrasting his own wicked people with these Lamanites, Mormon writes that "the church was broken up in all the land save it were among a few of the Lamanites who were converted unto the true faith; and they would not depart from it, for they were firm, and steadfast, and immovable, willing with all diligence to keep the commandments of the Lord" (3 Ne. 6:14). A helpful way to proceed, therefore, is with the question, What kind of unity does Mormon present as ideal, and what is the logic informing its approbation?

First, Mormon laments that several years before Christ's appearance to the Nephites, occupational specialization had led to his people being "distinguished by ranks" and "divided into classes" (3 Ne. 6:12; 4 Ne. 1:26). He does not argue that vertical social relationships are inherently evil so much as he condemns wealth-based social hierarchies, according to which the rich and advantaged are afforded a privileged status over the less advantaged. The implication seems to be that social relationships should be founded upon equality, civility, and mutual respect, independent of one's financial assets or vocational training. The challenge inherent in this proposition is the tendency to privilege what David Brooks, an American political commentator, calls the "résumé virtues" over a person's moral character.[8] Résumé virtues are those skills and advantages that one brings to the social marketplace: privileged upbringing, education, job training, physical ability and appearance, technical know-how, and so on. Mormon, however, implies that, while important for building a society, résumé virtues should not separate people vertically so much as they should differentiate them horizontally. In other words, his denigration of social hierarchies illustrates his preference for specialization with minimal stratification.

Mormon is equally critical of certain forms of tribalism, which he frames as a cause of wickedness, sedition, and contention among the people. He writes that prior to Christ's coming the people "were divided one against another; and they did separate one from another into tribes, every man according to his family and his kindred and friends" (3 Ne. 7:2). The reasons for their fracturing were many, including political ideology, religious beliefs, family traditions, lust for power and wealth, and resentment. Mormon argues that the kind of unity that overcomes such divisions is a shared commitment to protect human lives and "to maintain their rights, and the privileges of their church and of their worship, and their freedom and their liberty" (3 Ne. 2: 12). He also cites the commitment to defend and retain one's "property" and "country" (3 Ne. 3:2). These are among the shared cultural values that enabled the Nephites and Lamanites to join together in combatting the Gadianton robbers.

While Mormon certainly disparages social divisiveness, it may be argued that he also undermines the call to unity in that he appears reluctant to grant those who were originally Lamanites the full status of "Nephite" following their conversion to Christ. Early in 3 Nephi, for example, he mentions certain Lamanites who "had united with the Nephites," "were numbered among the Nephites," or "were called Nephites," yet when he speaks about them in later chapters, he still periodically refers to them as "Lamanites" or as "those who had been called Lamanites" (3 Ne. 2:12, 14, 16; 3:14; 6:14; 9:20; 10:18). Surely some of this ambivalence extends from his effort to demonstrate the Lord's power in softening the hearts of these people. In other words, by mentioning that previously wicked persons were now righteous, Mormon is able to demonstrate how the Lord, over time, granted the Lamanites "great favors" and how they had "great blessings poured out upon their heads" (3 Ne. 10:18).

At the same time, however, there is a sense in which preserving the title "Lamanite" for a newly minted Nephite conveys a subtle, albeit significant, message to the reader: this person is different. Modern analogies abound. Consider, for example, the tendency in the modern Church to distinguish between individuals born in the covenant and those who are converts to the Church, between persons of pioneer stock and those with no Latter-day Saint ancestry, between returned missionaries and those who did not serve a mission or came home early, or perhaps between "Utah Mormons" and those who live outside of Utah or the continental United States of America. While seemingly innocuous, such cultural designations may function as levers for marginalization. They may convey the message that those who do not fit the prototypical cultural molds are accepted by God not as legitimate children but as stepchildren, as addenda to the history of the Church but "never in the main text."[9] It is perhaps in response to this kind of thinking that Christ chastised the Nephites for not sufficiently preserving and valuing the teachings of Samuel the Lamanite (3 Ne. 23:6–13).

My intention here is not to suggest that Mormon intended to portray Lamanite converts as second-class

Nephites. Rather, it is merely to draw attention to the point that words matter in the project of forming unity. Seldom can we categorize people without also creating hierarchies or prescribing parameters for interaction that undermine Jesus's injunction of equality and universal love. It is telling that when Mormon describes Nephite society at the apex of its righteousness, he does away entirely with the language of tribal affiliation, saying that there were no Nephites or Lamanites, "nor any manner of -ites; but they were in one, the children of Christ, and heirs to the kingdom of God" (4 Ne. 1:17). Kinship with God and covenantal relationships transcend all earthly cultural identity.

A final form of unity mentioned in 3–4 Nephi is unity in worship. In several places, Mormon remarks that the people "gathered together" to teach, be taught, and participate in religious rituals (3 Ne. 11:1; 18:1–6; 19:4; 26:13, 16; 27:1). Christ also instructs the Nephites to "meet together oft" for similar purposes (3 Ne. 18:22). Mormon's emphasis on communal worship is linked to several convictions. The first is that Christ desires all persons to be saved. For this reason, he instructs the Nephites to "not forbid any man from coming unto you when ye shall meet together" (3 Ne. 18:22). Elsewhere he adds that while an unworthy person should be prohibited from receiving the sacrament, one should "not cast him out from among you, but ye shall minister unto him and shall pray for him unto the Father, in my name . . . for ye know not but what they will return and repent" (3 Ne. 18:30–32). Here the message seems to be that disciples of Christ are to imitate Christ's willingness to welcome all persons into community.

The second conviction underlying the importance of communal worship is that Christian discipleship entails serving and being served. As one thoughtful reverend has observed, "It is impossible to have a new relationship with God without also having a new relationship to people. The very first green tendril of love which sprouts in the human heart fumbles its way immediately toward the human other."[10] Mormon's emphasis on ethics, virtue, and the dangers of individualism and moral narcissism makes it clear that Christian discipleship does not offer a contemplative escape from life, a chance to be "spiritual" but not "religious." Worshipping God is a commitment to consistently confront the needs of others in all their sanctifying inconvenience. The disciple "works out the way to God by walking with others."[11]

Finally, Mormon seems to suggest that the power of worship and spiritual exercise may also become more efficacious by its collective performance. For this reason, when the Nephite disciples desired a special blessing from God, they "united in mighty prayer and fasting" (3 Ne. 27:1). Elsewhere, when the people desperately sought deliverance from their enemies, they similarly petitioned and praised God with "one voice" (3 Ne. 3:25; 4:8, 30–32). In these passages, unity appears to be a significant influence in attaining the desired outcome. It is certainly not uncommon in the modern Church for persons to engage in similar behavior: for families or congregations to join together in fasting and prayer for a sick person or a missionary or in response to a disaster. Speaking to this very phenomenon, one French clergyman wrote the following: "Private prayer is like straw scattered here and there: If you set it on fire it makes a lot of little flames. But gather these straws into a bundle and light them, and you get a mighty fire, rising like a column into the sky; public prayer is like that."[13]

I don't think the lesson that Mormon wishes to convey is that God cares all that much about his people doing the same thing at the same time. Rather, perhaps the lesson is that God is pleased with and honors the work accomplished in truly worshipping together. Communal prayer, for example, can attune one's heart not just to God but to one another. It demands that we are cognizant of others' needs and desires and that we care enough about them to muster the sincerity to truly pray with "one voice" (3 Ne. 20:9). It makes us vulnerable and more visible to one another. It demonstrates to God that we recognize that our relationship with him finds its fulfillment in our associations with one another.

Conclusion

I have framed this book as an effort to enlist 3–4 Nephi as aids in the disciple's pursuit of Christ and Christlikeness. I would like to conclude by briefly reflecting on three broad claims I have made. The first is that Mormon invites disciples to allow Christ to defy their expectations. He presents to us a Savior who resists easy categorization, who blurs the boundaries between humanity and divinity, between father and son, between male and female, and between individuality and relationality. We encounter a Savior who is at times present but not discernable or absent but not elsewhere. Mormon's multifaceted portrayal of Christ raises an important question for the disciple: Does my current understanding of the Savior ever prevent me from seeing the bigger picture? Or, put a slightly different way, Does what I already "know" ever limit what God can teach me?

If there is always more to know of Christ, and I believe there is, then discipleship must at times be coupled with a suspension of certainty. Certainty, I would argue, can be just as unproductive as unbelief if it stifles our openness to being surprised by Christ—by his love for the sinner, for example, or by his ability to relate to our unique circumstances, or by his desire to be involved in the minutia of our lives, or by his willingness to bless us when we don't think we deserve it. Such an openness is difficult because it requires us to take seriously the incompleteness of our knowledge, to question our assumptions, and to reevaluate our expectations. It demands that we become accustomed to ambiguity and doubt and that we embrace these things not as stumbling blocks in our journey of faith but as stepping-stones toward a more intimate knowledge of Christ.

Mormon reminds us that knowledge of Christ also requires the cultivation of moral character. In this sense, knowing the Savior is as much experiential as it is cognitive; we come to know him through our experience of becoming like him. To invoke the theologian Gregory of Nyssa again, as we mature spiritually, Christ reveals himself "in the mirror that we are," causing our souls to gleam "in company with the light that appears within it," thus making "the Invisible visible for us and the Incomprehensible comprehensible."[1] In the process of spiritual growth, the human soul becomes a medium through which Christ teaches us about himself. In our most noble moments, we can experience to some degree what it is to see, feel, and think like the Savior. Being one with him, we can know what it is to truly love a stranger, for instance, to forgive an enemy without reservation, or to abhor sin.

The theme of divine/human oneness in 3–4 Nephi reminds us that human and divine identity are relational, another claim I make in this book. This relationality also encompasses the idea that Christ sees himself in humans, a teaching perhaps most clearly articulated in Matthew 25, in which Christ, in the voice of a King, says:

> Come, ye blessed of my Father, inherit the kingdom prepared for you from the foundation of the world: For I was an hungred, and ye gave me meat: I was thirsty, and ye gave me drink: I was a stranger, and ye took me in: Naked, and ye clothed me: I was sick, and ye visited me: I was in prison, and ye came unto me. (Matt. 25:34–36)

Matthew records that at first the righteous deny that they have done any of these things for Jesus, to which the Savior responds: "Inasmuch as ye have done it unto one of the least of these my brethren, ye have done it unto me" (Matt. 25:40). In this passage Christ equates himself to the hungry, thirsty, stranger, naked, sick, and imprisoned (i.e., the "least of these").

It is significant that Jesus sees himself not just in anyone but in the marginalized and disadvantaged of society. On the one hand, this should motivate disciples to minister to the needy around them, as an expression of love not only to their neighbors but to the God who is reflected in them. In the voice of King Benjamin, Mormon makes explicit that "when ye are in the service of your fellow beings ye are only in the service of your God" (Mosiah 2:17). On the other hand, Christ's identification with the marginalized should also cause us to reflect on who he really was. He didn't just care for the poor; he was poor. He didn't just minister to ethnic minorities in the Roman Empire; he was one. He also was a refugee, was convicted of a crime, and was a victim of government-sanctioned oppression. In other words, Christ's ministry to the marginalized was not a charitable condescension to their level. From the day he was born to the day he died, he was one of them. Forgetting this risks inhibiting our ability to understand, love, serve, and see as equals those who are similarly marginalized in modern society.[2] There is power in trying to see Christ in those we are more accustomed to ignore or look down upon.

A final and related claim I would like to reflect on is the idea that coming unto Christ is a communal and collaborative endeavor. I believe that Mormon would have us understand that the path to the Savior is more circuitous and scenic than one might expect. In 3–4 Nephi, coming to Christ is what happens when the disciple focuses on other things. We make progress on the road not by speeding as quickly and efficiently as we can to our destination but by stopping to help others who have broken down along the way and by taking detours to search for those who are lost or stranded. As Martin Luther King Jr. once said, "I can never be what I ought to be until you are what you ought to be, and you can never be what you ought to be until I am what I ought to be."[3] Mormon's focus on other-centeredness and outward-orientation invites the disciple to see salvation less as a goal that can be sought out for its own sake and more as a byproduct of trying to love and serve others. It is the accumulation of small and simple things made great by God.

Further Reading

introduction

For a general introduction to the study and development of Christian theology:

Alister E. McGrath, *Christian Theology: An Introduction*, 6th ed. (Oxford: Wiley-Blackwell, 2016)

Alister E. McGrath, ed., *The Christian Theology Reader*, 5th ed. (Oxford: Wiley-Blackwell, 2016).

For an introduction to some prominent themes and theological topics in 3 Nephi:

Andrew C. Skinner and Gaye Strathearn, eds., *Third Nephi: An Incomparable Scripture* (Salt Lake City and Provo, UT: Deseret Book and Neal A. Maxwell Institute for Religious Scholarship, 2011).

chapter 1

For more on the portrayal of Christ in the Book of Mormon and Latter-day Saint thought:

John G. Turner, *The Mormon Jesus: A Biography* (Cambridge, MA: Harvard University Press, 2016).

For more on the sacrament prayers in 3 Nephi and Moroni:

John W. Welch, "From Presence to Practice: Jesus, the Sacrament Prayers, the Priesthood, and Church Discipline in 3 Nephi 18 and Moroni 2–6," *Journal of Book of Mormon Studies* 5, no. 1 (1996): 119–39.

chapter 2

On the topic of race as it relates to the Book of Mormon:

Kimberly Berkey and Joseph Spencer, "'Great Cause to Mourn': The Complexity of *The Book of Mormon*'s Presentation of Gender and Race," in *Americanist Approaches to the Book of Mormon*, ed. Elizabeth Fenton and Jared Hickman (New York: Oxford University Press, 2019), 298–320.

Ignacio Garcia, "Thoughts on Latino Mormons, Their Afterlife, and the Need for a New Historical Paradigm for Saints of Color," *Dialogue* 50, no. 4 (2017): 1–30.

Patrick Q. Mason, "Mormonism and Race," in *The Oxford Handbook of Religion and Race in American History*, ed. Kathryn Gin Lum and Paul Harvey (New York: Oxford University Press, 2018), 160–163

Russell W. Stevenson, "Reckoning with Race in the Book of Mormon: A Review of Literature," *Journal of Book of Mormon Studies* 27 (2018), 210–25.

chapter 3

For more on Jesus's sermon to the Nephites and how it relates to the New Testament:

Nicholas J. Frederick, "The Book of Mormon and Its Redaction of the King James New Testament," *Journal of Book of Mormon Studies* 27 (2018): 44–87.

George B. Handley, "Reading and the Menardian Paradox in 3 Nephi," *Journal of Book of Mormon Studies* 26 (2017): 165–84; Sidney B. Sperry, "The Book of Mormon and the Problem of the Sermon on the Mount," Journal of Book of Mormon Studies 4, no. 1 (1995): 153–65.

Krister Stendahl, "The Sermon on the Mount and Third Nephi," in *Reflections on Mormonism: Judaeo-Christian Parallels*, ed. Truman G. Madsen (Provo,

UT: Religious Studies Center, Brigham Young
University, 1978), 139–54.

John Welch, *The Sermon at the Temple and the Sermon
on the Mount: A Latter-day Saint Approach* (Salt
Lake City, UT: Deseret Book, 1990).

chapter 4

For more on political discourse in the Book of Mormon:

David Charles Gore, *The Voice of the People: Political
Rhetoric in the Book of Mormon* (Provo, UT: Neal A.
Maxwell Institute for Religious Scholarship, 2019).

Endnotes

SERIES INTRODUCTION

1. Elder Neal A. Maxwell, "The Children of Christ," university devotional, Brigham Young University, Provo, UT, 4 February 1990, https://speeches.byu.edu/talks/neal–a–maxwell_children–christ/.

2. Elder Neal A. Maxwell, "The Inexhaustible Gospel," university devotional, Brigham Young University, Provo, UT, 18 August 1992, https://speeches.byu.edu/talks/neal–a–maxwell/ inexhaustible–gospel/.

3. Elder Neal A. Maxwell, "The Book of Mormon: A Great Answer to 'The Great Question,'" address, Book of Mormon Symposium, Brigham Young University, Provo, UT, 10 October 1986, reprinted in *The Voice of My Servants: Apostolic Messages on Teaching, Learning, and Scripture,* ed. Scott C. Esplin and Richard Neitzel Holzapfel (Provo, UT: Religious Studies Center, Brigham Young University; Salt Lake City: Deseret Book, 2010), 221–38, https://rsc.byu.edu/archived/ voice–my–servants/book–mormon–great–answer–great–question.

INTRODUCTION

1. I am grateful for the numerous people who have provided research help and feedback on this volume as it was taking shape: Emily Becerra, my parents, Savannah Burgoyne, Rachel Carter, Jason Combs, Ignacio Garcia, Nicole Gurley, John Hilton, Kristian Heal, Dan Judd, Daniel Nelson, Meridith Reed, Ryan Sharp, Joseph Spencer, Charles Swift, and Catherine Taylor.

1

1. Origen, *Against Celsus* 3.45, in *Contra Celsum*, trans. Henry Chadwick (Cambridge: Cambridge University Press, 1980), 159–60.

2. Gregory of Nazianzus, *Letter* 101.32, in *Nicene and Post-Nicene Fathers*, 2nd ser., trans. Charles Browne and James Swallow (Peabody, MA: Hendrickson, 1994), 7:440.

3. Andrew C. Skinner, "Jesus Christ as Father in the Book of Mormon," in *The Fulness of the Gospel: Foundational Teachings from the Book of Mormon*, ed. Camille Fronk Olson, Brian M. Hauglid, Patty Smith, and Thomas A. Wayment (Provo, UT; Religious Studies Center, 2003), 134–149.

4. Letter of *Ammonas* 9, in *The Letters of Ammonas*, trans. Derwas Chitty (Oxford, UK: SLG Press, 2017), 12–13.

5. Jane Allis-Pike, "'How Oft Would I Have Gathered You as a Hen Gathereth Her Chickens': The Power of the Hen Metaphor in 3 Nephi 10: 4–7," in *Third Nephi: An Incomparable Scripture*, ed. Andrew C. Skinner and Gaye Strathearn (Salt Lake City and Provo, UT: Deseret Book and Neal A. Maxwell Institute for Religious Scholarship, 2012), 57–74.

6. Gregory of Nazianzus, *Oration* 6.13, in *The Fathers of the Church*, trans. Martha Vinson (Washington DC: Catholic University Press), 107:13–14.

7. Gregory of Nazianzus, *Oration* 6.4, in *Fathers*, trans. Vinson, 107:6.

2

1. I have not included "bowels" here, which appear eight times in the Book of Mormon. Bowels do seat some emotional expressions, such as mercy and compassion (Mosiah 15:9; Alma 7:12; 26:37; 34:15; 3 Ne. 17:6–7). Only Christ's bowels, however, function like this. No human bowels appear to perform psychological functions.

2. David Bednar, "The Atonement and Journey of Mortality" *Ensign*, April 2012, 40.

3. Fr. Gregory Boyle on *I Love You, America, with Sarah Silverman*, season 1, episode 5, "Father Greg Boyle," directed by Allan Kartun, presented by Sarah Silverman, aired November 9, 2017, on Hulu.

4. On the relationship of authenticity and morality, see Derek Phillips, "Authenticity or Morality?" in *The Virtues: Contemporary*

Essays on Moral Character, eds. Robert B. Kruschwitz and Robert C. Roberts (Belmont, CA: Wadsworth, 1987), 23–35.

5. For a representative example of what I understand to be a positive use of the rhetoric of "authenticity" in modern Latter-day Saint discourse, see Dan Wotherspoon, "Being Authentic within Mormonism," September 23, 2014, episodes 249–50 of *Mormon Matters*, podcast, https://www.mormon-matters.org/podcast-item/249-250-being-authentic-within-mormonism/.

6. Phillips, "Authenticity or Morality?" 24.

7. On Latter-day Saint responses to discussions of race in the Book of Mormon, see Russell W. Stevenson, "Reckoning with Race in the Book of Mormon: A Review of Literature," *Journal of Book of Mormon Studies (JBMS)* 27 (2018): 210–25.

8. Rodney Turner, "The Lamanite Mark," in The Book of Mormon: *Second Nephi, the Doctrinal Structure*, ed. Monte S. Nyman and Charles D. Tate Jr. (Provo, UT: Religious Studies Center, Brigham Young University, 1989), 133–57.

9. Amy Easton-Flake, "Lehi's Dream as a Template for Understanding Each Act of Nephi's Vision," in *The Things Which My Father Saw: Approaches to Lehi's Dream and Nephi's Vision*, 2011 Sperry Symposium, ed. Daniel L. Belnap, Gaye Strathearn, and Stanley A. Johnson (Provo, UT: Religious Studies Center, Brigham Young University; Salt Lake City: Deseret Book, 2011), 179–98; Thomas W. Murphy, "Sin, Skin, and Seed: Mistakes of Men in the Book of Mormon," *The John Whitmer Historical Association Journal* 25 (2005): 36–51; Steven Olsen, "The Covenant of the Chosen People: The Spiritual Foundations of Ethnic Identity in the Book of Mormon," *JBMS* 21, no. 2 (2012): 14–29; Adam O. Stokes, "'Skin' or 'Scales' of Blackness? Semitic Context as Interpretive Aid for 2 Nephi 4:35 (LDS 5:21)" *JBMS* 27 (2018): 278–289.

10. Ethan Sproat, "Skin as Garments in the Book of Mormon: A Textual Exegesis," *JBMS* 24, no. 1 (2015); 138–65.

11. For Sproat's response to this kind of reading, see "Skin as Garments," 161–63.

12. I am indebted to Patrick Mason for this observation. See "Race and the Book of Mormon," in *The Oxford Handbook of Religion and Race in American History*, ed. Kathryn Gin Lum and Paul Harvey (New York: Oxford University Press, 2018), 162.

13. Mason, "Race and the Book of Mormon," 162.

14. Richard Lyman Bushman, *Joseph Smith: Rough Stone Rolling* (New York: Knopf, Vintage, 2005), 98.

15. Jared Hickman, "*The Book of Mormon* as Amerindian Apocalypse," *American Literature* 86, no. 3 (2014): 446–7, 451, 454.

16. Lactantius, *Divine Institutes* 6.10., in *The Christian Theology Reader*, trans. Allister McGrath (Oxford: Wiley-Blackwell, 2016), 345.

3

1. My language here is indebted to Patout Burns, *The Development of the Augustine's Doctrine of Operative Grace* (Paris: Études augustiniennes, 1980), 82–82.

2. Although I am defining it differently, this term appears in Daniel Harrington and James Keenan, *Jesus and Virtue Ethics: Building Bridges between New Testament Studies and Moral Theology* (Oxford: Rowman and Littlefield, 2002), 3.

3. Robert Browne, "Piety," in *Traditional Virtues Reassessed*, ed. A. R. Vidler (London: SPCK, 1964), 35.

4. I am indebted to Joan Chittister for this insight. See Chittister, *The Rule of Benedict: A Spirituality for the 21st Century* (New York: Crossroad, 2016), 28.

5. Narsai, Memra *27 on the Parable of the Ten Virgins* 400–403. This is my translation. No published English translation currently exists. For the Syriac edition see Alphonsi Mingana (ed.), *Narsai Homiliae et carmina* (Mosul, Iraq: Fraternity of Preachers, 1905), 1:257.

6. Gregory of Nyssa, *Homilies on the Song of Songs* (Homily 4), trans. Richard Norris (Atlanta, GA: Society of Biblical Literature, 2013), 113.

7. Joseph F. Smith, *Teachings of the Prophet Joseph Smith* (Salt Lake City, UT: Deseret Book, 1993), 268.

8. Tim Cook, ed., *The Poems of Robert Browning* (London: Wordsworth Poetry Library, 1994), 442.

9. For more on toxic perfectionism, see Jane Clayson Johnson, *Silent Souls Weeping: Depression: Sharing Stories, Finding Hope* (Salt Lake City, UT: Deseret Book, 2018), 52–74.

10. Frances Young, *God's Presence: A Contemporary Recapitulation of Early Christianity* (Cambridge: Cambridge University Press, 2013), 37–39.

11. Gregory of Nyssa, *Homilies on the Song of Songs* (Homily 8), trans. Richard Norris (Atlanta: Society of Biblical Literature, 2013), 261.

12. Brett P. Thomas, "They Did Remember His Words," in *The Book of Mormon: Helaman through 3 Nephi 8: According to Thy Word*, ed. Monte S. Lyman and Charles D. Tate (Provo, UT: Religious Studies Center, 1992), 93–114.

13. Arthur Schopenhauer, *The Basis of Morality* (New York: Macmillan, 1915), 170.

14. H. G. Frankfurt, "Freedom of the Will and the Concept of a Person," *The Journal of Philosophy* 68, no. 1 (1971): 5–20.

4

1. (Eugene, OR: Pickwick, 2017). On the relationship between atonement and economic equality, see Lindon J. Robison, "No Poor Among Them," *Journal of Book of Mormon Studies* 14, no. 1 (Provo, UT: Neal A. Maxwell Institute for Religious Scholarship, 2005): 86–97, 130.

2. King Benjamin would add that if persons do not have access to wealth, they should be able to say in their hearts, "I give not because I have not, but if I had I would give" (Mosiah 4:24). On the virtue of generosity, see James Wallace, "Generosity," in *Vice and Virtue in Everyday Life: Introductory Readings in Ethics*, 3rd ed., ed. Christina Sommers and Fred Sommers (Fort Worth, TX: Harcourt Brace Jovanovich, 1993), 288–295.

3. Jerome, *Against Jovinan* 1.12 (PL 23.228), this is my translation; cf. Jerome, *Against Jovinan* 1.12 in *Nicene and Post-Nicene Fathers*, 2nd ser., trans. W. H. Fremantle, G. Lewis, and W. G. Martley (Peabody, MA: Hendrickson, 1994), 6:355.

4. Evagrius, *Alphabetic Maxims* 2.16, in *Evargius of Pontus: The Greek Ascetics Corpus*, trans. Robert Sinkewicz (Oxford: Oxford University Press, 2006), 231.

5. Quoted in Preston Nibley, *Brigham Young: The Man and His Work* (Salt Lake City, UT: Deseret News Press, 1936), 128.

6. John Chrysostom, *Homilies on the Gospel of Matthew* 87.4 in *Social Thought*, Message of the Fathers of the Church 20, trans. Peter Phan (Wilmington, DE: Michael Glazier, 1984), 146.

7. Jonathan Haidt, *The Righteous Mind: Why Good People Are Divided by Politics and Religion* (New York: Vintage Books, 2012), 105.

9. David Brooks, *The Road to Character* (New York: Random House, 2015), xi.

10. Ignacio M. Garcia, "Thoughts on Latino Mormons, Their Afterlife, and the Need for a New Historical Paradigm for Saints of Color" *Dialogue: A Journal of Mormon Thought* 50, no. 4 (Winter 2017): 1–30. doi:10.5406/dialjmormthou.50.4.0001

11. Karl A. Olsson, *Seven Sins and Seven Virtues* (New York: Harper and Brothers, 1962), 119.

12. Joan Chittister, *The Rule of Benedict: A Spirituality for the 21st Century* (New York: Crossroad, 2016), 27.

13. Quote of John Vianney in John Cumming, ed., *Butler's Lives of the Saints* (Collegeville, MN: Burns & Oates, 1998), 31.

CONCLUSION

1. Gregory of Nyssa, *Homilies on the Song of Songs* (Homilies 3, 4), trans. Richard Norris (Atlanta: Society of Biblical Literature, 2012), 101, 115.

2. My argument in this paragraph is indebted to Christena Cleveland, "Why Jesus' Skin Color Matters," *Christianity Today*, March 18, 2016, 36.

3. Martin Luther King, *Strength to love* (Minneapolis, MN: Fortress, 2010), 69.

Editions of the
Book of Mormon

Most Latter-day Saints are familiar principally with the official edition of the Book of Mormon published in 2013 by The Church of Jesus Christ of Latter-day Saints. It contains the canonical text of the book, divided into chapters of relatively even length with numbered verses for ease of access. Its footnotes aim to assist readers in seeking doctrinal understanding.

Other Book of Mormon editions are available and often helpful. Among these are official editions from earlier in the scripture's publishing history, which are relatively accessible. There are also editions published recently by a variety of presses meant to make the text more readable. Both types of editions are referred to throughout *Book of Mormon: brief theological introductions*. Also of importance (and occasionally referred to) are the manuscript sources for the printed editions of the Book of Mormon.

manuscript sources

Unfortunately, the original manuscript of the Book of Mormon was damaged during the nineteenth century, but substantial portions of it remain. All known extant portions have been published in typescript in Royal Skousen, ed., *The Original Manuscript of the Book of Mormon: Typographical Facsimile of the Extant Text* (Provo, UT: Foundation for Ancient Research and Mormon Studies [FARMS], 2001). A future volume of the Joseph Smith Papers will publish images of the extant manuscript, along with a typescript.

After completing the original manuscript's dictation, Joseph Smith assigned Oliver Cowdery to produce a second manuscript copy of the text. That manuscript has been called the printer's manuscript since it was designed for use by the first printer of the Book of Mormon. The printer's manuscript, which is more or less entirely intact, also contains corrections and other editorial markings inserted when the second (1837) edition of the Book of Mormon was being prepared. A typescript of the printer's manuscript can be found in Royal Skousen, ed., *The Printer's Manuscript of the Book of Mormon: Typographical Facsimile of the Entire Text in Two Parts,*

2 vols. (Provo, UT: FARMS, 2001). Full color images of the manuscript were subsequently published along with a transcript in the Joseph Smith Papers: Royal Skousen and Robin Scott Jensen, eds., *Printer's Manuscript of the Book of Mormon*, 2 parts, Revelations and Translations 3 (Salt Lake City: Church Historian's Press, 2015). The images and transcript of the printer's manuscript are also available at the Joseph Smith Papers website (www.josephsmithpapers.org/the-papers/revelations-and-translations/jsppr3).

historical editions

Multiple editions of the Book of Mormon were published during the lifetime of Joseph Smith. The first edition, published in Palmyra, New York, in 1830, appeared without versification and with fewer chapter divisions than the present canonical text (see FIGURE 8). The text of the 1830 edition is available electronically at the Joseph Smith Papers website (www.josephsmithpapers.org/the-papers/revelations-and-translations/jsppr4) and in print through various publishers as a replica edition. The 1830 text is also available in Robert A. Rees and Eugene England, eds., *The Reader's Book of Mormon* (Salt Lake City, UT: Signature Books, 2008), which is divided into seven pocket-sized volumes (each with an introduction by a scholar).

Joseph Smith introduced numerous minor changes into the text of the Book of Mormon when it was prepared for a second edition in 1837. Many of these changes are marked in the printer's manuscript. Most were aimed at correcting grammatical issues, but some, in a small handful of cases, were also aimed at clarifying the meaning of the text or its doctrinal implications. The 1837 edition is available electronically at the Joseph Smith Papers website (www.josephsmithpapers.org/the-papers/revelations-and-translations/jsppr4).

A third edition was prepared under Joseph Smith's direction in 1840, and evidence makes clear that the original manuscript was consulted carefully in preparing this edition. Some important errors in the earlier editions were corrected, further grammatical improvements were introduced, and a few other changes were made to the text for purposes of clarification. The 1840 edition can be read at the Joseph Smith Papers website (www.josephsmithpapers.org/the-papers/revelations-and-translations/jsppr4). It forms the basis for at least one printed edition as well: *The Book of Mormon*, trans. Joseph Smith Jr. (New York: Penguin Books, 2008), which contains a helpful introduction by Laurie Maffly-Kipp, a scholar of American religious history.

THE

BOOK OF MORMON:

AN ACCOUNT WRITTEN BY THE HAND OF MOR-MON, UPON PLATES TAKEN FROM THE PLATES OF NEPHI.

Wherefore it is an abridgment of the Record of the People of Nephi; and also of the Lamanites; written to the Lamanites, which are a remnant of the House of Israel; and also to Jew and Gentile; written by way of commandment, and also by the spirit of Prophesy and of Revelation. Written, and sealed up, and hid up unto the LORD, that they might not be destroyed; to come forth by the gift and power of GOD unto the interpretation thereof; sealed by the hand of Moroni, and hid up unto the LORD, to come forth in due time by the way of Gentile; the interpretation thereof by the gift of GOD; an abridgment taken from the Book of Ether.

Also, which is a Record of the People of Jared, which were scattered at the time the LORD confounded the language of the people when they were building a tower to get to Heaven: which is to shew unto the remnant of the House of Israel how great things the LORD hath done for their fathers; and that they may know the covenants of the LORD, that they are not cast off forever; and also to the convincing of the Jew and Gentile that JESUS is the CHRIST, the ETERNAL GOD, manifesting Himself unto all nations. And now if there be fault, it he the mistake of men; wherefore condemn not the things of GOD, that ye may be found spotless at the judgment seat of CHRIST.

BY JOSEPH SMITH, JUNIOR,

AUTHOR AND PROPRIETOR.

PALMYRA:

PRINTED BY E. B. GRANDIN, FOR THE AUTHOR.

1830.

FIGURE 8   The title page of the original 1830 edition of The Book of Mormon. © Intellectual Reserve, Inc.

One other edition of the Book of Mormon appeared during the lifetime of Joseph Smith—an 1841 British edition, which was largely based on the 1837 edition and therefore lacked corrections and other improvements that appear in the 1840 edition. It, too, is available electronically at the Joseph Smith Papers website (www.josephsmithpapers.org/the-papers/revelations-and-translations/jsppr4).

In 1879, Latter-day Saint apostle Orson Pratt completed one of the more influential editions of the Book of Mormon published after Joseph Smith's death. Pratt lamented that too many Latter-day Saints left the scripture unread on the shelf. He sought to create an easier reading experience by dividing up the originally long chapters and adding verse numbers—revisions which have largely remained unchanged in the Church's official edition to the present. He also pioneered a system of cross-references and other explanatory footnotes. Most of Pratt's notes were removed or replaced in subsequent official editions—most thoroughly in the Church's 1981 edition when new descriptive chapter headings were introduced. These headings can still be found, with a few minor updates, in the 2013 edition.

A detailed and helpful devotional treatment of the publication history of the Book of Mormon can be found in Richard E. Turley, Jr. and William W. Slaughter, *How We Got the Book of Mormon* (Salt Lake City: Deseret Book, 2011). These authors trace developments in the format and study apparatuses used to present the text of the Book of Mormon to audiences from the 1850s to the present.

study and reading editions
The most important scholarly editions of the Book of Mormon are Grant Hardy, ed., *The Book of Mormon: A Reader's Edition* (Urbana and Chicago: University of Illinois Press, 2003); and Royal Skousen, ed., *The Book of Mormon: The Earliest Text* (New Haven, CT: Yale University Press, 2009).

Hardy's edition repackages the text of the 1921 public domain edition of the Book of Mormon. It contains a helpful introduction, a series of useful appendices, and a straightforward presentation of the text in a highly readable format. Footnotes are minimal—they are used only to clarify direct references or allusions within the text, to track dates, or to alert readers about original chapter divisions. This edition contains modern chapter and verse divisions, but they are unobtrusively typeset. The text is presented in straightforward paragraphs, with one-line headings marking text divisions. Poetry is set off in poetic lines, as in modern editions of the Bible.

Skousen's edition is the result of his quarter-century-long work with the manuscript and printed sources for the Book of Mormon text. The edition aims to reproduce as closely as can be reconstructed the words originally dictated by Joseph Smith to his scribes. Chapter and verse divisions familiar from recent editions are in the text (and symbols mark original chapter breaks), but the text is presented in what Skousen calls "sense lines"—each line containing (on Skousen's reconstruction) approximately what the prophet would have dictated at one time before pausing to allow his scribe to write. The edition contains helpful introductory material and a summary appendix noting significant differences between *The Earliest Text* and the current official edition. It is otherwise without any apparatus for the reader.

The most significant edition of the Book of Mormon deliberately constructed for a lay reading audience is Grant Hardy, ed., *The Book of Mormon: Another Testament of Jesus Christ,* Maxwell Institute Study Edition (Salt Lake City and Provo, UT: Neal A. Maxwell Institute for Religious Scholarship, Deseret Book, and BYU Religious Studies Center, 2018). In this edition, Hardy uses the text of the 2013 official edition of the Book of Mormon but presents it in a readable way for everyday students of the volume. This edition reproduces the best of what appears in Hardy's *Reader's Edition* but adds further resources in the introductory and appendix materials. The footnotes are updated and expanded to include variant readings from the original and printer's manuscripts, and to provide notes about other textual details. The body of the text is presented, as in the *Reader's Edition*, in a straightforward fashion, readable and interrupted only by one-line headings. Modern chapter and verse divisions, as well as original chapter divisions, are easily visible.

Index

112

Colophon

The text of the book is typeset in Arnhem,
Fred Smeijer's 21st-century-take on late
18th-century Enlightenment-era letterforms
known for their sturdy legibility and clarity
of form. Captions and figures are typset in
Quaadraat Sans, also by Fred Smeijers.
The book title and chapter titles are typeset
in Thema by Nikola Djurek.

Printed on Domtar Lynx 74 gsm,
Forest Stewardship Council (FSC) Certified.

Printed by Brigham Young University Print & Mail Services

Woodcut illuminations Brian Kershisnik
Illumination consultation Faith Heard

Book design & typography Douglas Thomas
Production typesetting Sage Perez, Maria Camargo
Chart design Sage Perez, Maria Camargo, Douglas Thomas

3 Nephi 11:15 And it came to pass that the multitude went forth, and thrust their hands into his side, and did feel the prints of the nails in his hands and in his feet; and this they did do, going forth one by one until they had all gone forth, and did see with their eyes and did feel with their hands, and did know of a surety and did bear record, that it was he, of whom it was written by the prophets, that should come.